2015

all our love,

Leigh, Michael,
Morgen, Matt
and Mitch.

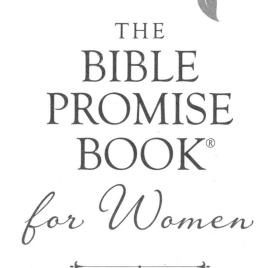

THE
BIBLE
PROMISE
BOOK®
for Women

+ • +

Prayer & Praise
Edition

BARBOUR
PUBLISHING

© 2014 by Barbour Publishing, Inc.

Print ISBN: 978-1-62836-645-7
Special Edition ISBN: 978-1-63058-359-0

eBook Editions:
Adobe Digital Edition (.epub) 978-1-63058-079-7
Kindle and MobiPocket Edition (.prc) 978-1-63058-080-3

All scripture quotations are taken from the King James Version of the Bible.

Published by Barbour Publishing, Inc., P.O. Box 719, Uhrichsville, Ohio 44683, www.barbourbooks.com

Our mission is to publish and distribute inspirational products offering exceptional value and biblical encouragement to the masses.

ecpa Member of the
Evangelical Christian
Publishers Association

Printed in China.

Introduction

Whatever the need of the moment, the answer is to be found in scripture, if we take the time to search for it. Whatever we're feeling, whatever we're suffering, whatever we're hoping, the Bible has something to say to us.

This collection of Bible verses, prayers, and hymn lyrics is meant to refresh and encourage you, no matter your struggle. Each section opens with a prayer written specifically for that topic and closes with praises from a relevant hymn. It is in no way intended to replace regular Bible study or the use of a concordance for in-depth study of a subject. There are many facets of your life and many topics in the Bible that are not covered here.

But if, for example, you are feeling extremely lonely one day, some of the Bible's wisdom and comfort is available to you here under the topic of *Loneliness*. All topics are arranged alphabetically for ease of use.

All scripture is from the King James Version of the Bible.

Contents

ANGER

---

*Dear Lord, when I let my emotions run
away from me and am overcome with anger,
remind me to take a deep breath and
follow the example You have given—one
of gentleness, mercy, and self-control. Amen.*

The LORD is gracious, and full of compassion;
slow to anger, and of great mercy.
PSALM 145:8

A God ready to pardon, gracious and merciful,
slow to anger, and of great kindness. . .
NEHEMIAH 9:17

For his anger endureth but a moment;
in his favour is life: weeping may endure for
a night, but joy cometh in the morning.
PSALM 30:5

Wherefore, my beloved brethren,
let every man be swift to hear, slow to speak,
slow to wrath: for the wrath of man
worketh not the righteousness of God.
JAMES 1:19–20

Be not hasty in thy spirit to be angry:
for anger resteth in the bosom of fools.
ECCLESIASTES 7:9

He that is soon angry dealeth foolishly.
PROVERBS 14:17

He that is slow to anger is better than the mighty;
and he that ruleth his spirit than he that taketh a city.
PROVERBS 16:32

A wrathful man stirreth up strife:
but he that is slow to anger appeaseth strife.
PROVERBS 15:18

An angry man stirreth up strife,
and a furious man aboundeth in transgression.
PROVERBS 29:22

Cease from anger, and forsake wrath:
fret not thyself in any wise to do evil.
PSALM 37:8

Amidst Thy wrath remember love,
Restore Thy servant, Lord;
Nor let a Father's chastening prove
Like an avenger's sword.

"AMIDST THY WRATH REMEMBER LOVE," ISAAC WATTS

Make no friendship with an angry man;
and with a furious man thou shalt not go:
lest thou learn his ways, and get a snare to thy soul.
PROVERBS 22:24–25

A soft answer turneth away wrath:
but grievous words stir up anger.
PROVERBS 15:1

Fathers, provoke not your children to anger,
lest they be discouraged.
COLOSSIANS 3:21

Be ye angry, and sin not:
let not the sun go down upon your wrath.
EPHESIANS 4:26

The discretion of a man deferreth his anger;
and it is his glory to pass over a transgression.

PROVERBS 19:11

It is better to dwell in the wilderness,
than with a contentious and an angry woman.

PROVERBS 21:19

But I say unto you, That whosoever is
angry with his brother without a cause shall
be in danger of the judgment.

MATTHEW 5:22

Let all bitterness, and wrath, and anger,
and clamour, and evil speaking, be put away from you,
with all malice: and be ye kind one to another,
tenderhearted, forgiving one another, even as
God for Christ's sake hath forgiven you.

EPHESIANS 4:31–32

Wrath is cruel, and anger is outrageous;
but who is able to stand before envy?

PROVERBS 27:4

If thine enemy be hungry, give him bread to eat;
and if he be thirsty, give him water to drink:
For thou shalt heap coals of fire upon his head,
and the LORD shall reward thee.

PROVERBS 25:21–22

Dearly beloved, avenge not yourselves,
but rather give place unto wrath: for it is written,
Vengeance is mine; I will repay, saith the Lord.
Therefore if thine enemy hunger, feed him;
if he thirst, give him drink: for in so doing thou
shalt heap coals of fire on his head. Be not
overcome of evil, but overcome evil with good.
ROMANS 12:19–21

But now ye also put off all these; anger, wrath, malice,
blasphemy, filthy communication out of your mouth.
COLOSSIANS 3:8

Hour by hour we hear a warning
From the spirit-voice within;
Hour by hour we meet the tempter,
Hour by hour we fall or win.

"HOUR BY HOUR," FANNY CROSBY

BELIEF

*Dear Lord, thank You for the certainty
that I have in You and for the ways
that You continually take care of me.
Even when I go through times of doubt,
remind me of all the ways You have
been faithful to me in the past and will
continue to be faithful in the future. Amen.*

For God so loved the world, that he gave his only
begotten Son, that whosoever believeth in him
should not perish, but have everlasting life.
JOHN 3:16

To him give all the prophets witness,
that through his name whosoever believeth
in him shall receive remission of sins.
ACTS 10:43

As it is written, Behold, I lay in Sion a
stumblingstone and rock of offence: and whosoever
believeth on him shall not be ashamed.
ROMANS 9:33

But as many as received him, to them gave
he power to become the sons of God,
even to them that believe on his name.
JOHN 1:12

He that believeth on him is not condemned:
but he that believeth not is condemned already,
because he hath not believed in the name of
the only begotten Son of God.
JOHN 3:18

He that believeth on the Son hath everlasting life:
and he that believeth not the Son shall not see life;
but the wrath of God abideth on him.
JOHN 3:36

Only believe, only believe;
All things are possible, only believe.
Fear not, little flock, whatever your lot,
He enters all rooms, the doors being shut;
He never forsakes, He never is gone,
So count on His presence in darkness and dawn.

"ONLY BELIEVE," PAUL RADER

Wherefore also it is contained in the scripture,
Behold, I lay in Sion a chief corner stone, elect, precious:
and he that believeth on him shall not be confounded.
1 Peter 2:6

And they said, Believe on the Lord Jesus Christ,
and thou shalt be saved, and thy house.
Acts 16:31

I am come a light into the world,
that whosoever believeth on me
should not abide in darkness.
John 12:46

And Jesus said unto them, I am the bread of life:
he that cometh to me shall never hunger;
and he that believeth on me shall never thirst.
John 6:35

Jesus said unto him, If thou canst believe,
all things are possible to him that believeth.
Mark 9:23 Jesus saith unto him, Thomas, because thou hast
seen me, thou hast believed: blessed are they
that have not seen, and yet have believed.
John 20:29

Verily, verily, I say unto you,
He that believeth on me hath everlasting life.
John 6:47

Lord, I believe: help Thou mine unbelief;
Let me no other master know but Thee.
Thou art the Christian's God,
the only King and Chief
Of all who soldiers of the cross would be.

"LORD, I BELIEVE," DANIEL HOWARD

CHARITY

—◆— · —◆—

Thank You for the blessings that
You have given me, Lord.
Make my heart sensitive to
the needs of those around me,
and let me unselfishly share what
You have blessed me with. Amen.

Blessed is he that considereth the poor:
the LORD will deliver him in time of trouble.
The LORD will preserve him, and keep him alive;
and he shall be blessed upon the earth: and thou wilt
not deliver him unto the will of his enemies.
PSALM 41:1–2

He that hath pity upon the poor lendeth
unto the LORD; and that which he hath given
will he pay him again.
PROVERBS 19:17

But when thou makest a feast, call the poor, the maimed,
the lame, the blind: and thou shalt be blessed;
for they cannot recompense thee: for thou shalt
be recompensed at the resurrection of the just.
LUKE 14:13–14

Sell that ye have, and give alms;
provide yourselves bags which wax not old,
a treasure in the heavens that faileth not,
where no thief approacheth, neither moth corrupteth.
LUKE 12:33

He that despiseth his neighbour sinneth:
but he that hath mercy on the poor, happy is he.
PROVERBS 14:21

Give, and it shall be given unto you; good measure,
pressed down, and shaken together, and running over,
shall men give into your bosom. For with the same measure
that ye mete withal it shall be measured to you again.
LUKE 6:38

He hath dispersed, he hath given to the poor;
his righteousness endureth for ever;
his horn shall be exalted with honour.
PSALM 112:9

And now abideth faith, hope, charity, these three;
but the greatest of these is charity.
1 CORINTHIANS 13:13

He that giveth unto the poor shall not lack:
but he that hideth his eyes shall have many a curse.
PROVERBS 28:27

Every man according as he purposeth in his heart,
so let him give; not grudgingly, or of necessity:
for God loveth a cheerful giver.
2 CORINTHIANS 9:7

Awake, my zeal; awake, my love,
To serve my Savior here below,
In works which perfect saints above
And holy angels cannot do.

Awake, my charity, to feed
The hungry soul, and clothe the poor;
In Heav'n are found no sons of need,
There all these duties are no more.

"AWAKE, MY ZEAL; AWAKE, MY LOVE," ISAAC WATTS

There is that scattereth, and yet increaseth;
and there is that withholdeth more than is meet,
but it tendeth to poverty. The liberal soul shall be made fat:
and he that watereth shall be watered also himself.
PROVERBS 11:24–25

I have been young, and now am old;
yet have I not seen the righteous forsaken,
nor his seed begging bread.
PSALM 37:25

Charge them that are rich in this world,
that they be not highminded, nor trust in uncertain riches,
but in the living God, who giveth us richly all things to enjoy;
that they do good, that they be rich in good works,
ready to distribute, willing to communicate.
1 TIMOTHY 6:17–18

Cast thy bread upon the waters:
for thou shalt find it after many days.
ECCLESIASTES 11:1

And if thou draw out thy soul to the hungry,
and satisfy the afflicted soul;
then shall thy light rise in obscurity,
and thy darkness be as the noon day.
ISAIAH 58:10

Is it not to deal thy bread to the hungry,
and that thou bring the poor that are cast out to thy house?
when thou seest the naked, that thou cover him;
and that thou hide not thyself from thine own flesh?
Then shall thy light break forth as the morning,
and thine health shall spring forth speedily:
and thy righteousness shall go before thee;
the glory of the LORD shall be thy reward.

ISAIAH 58:7–8

And the Levite, (because he hath no
part nor inheritance with thee,)
and the stranger, and the fatherless,
and the widow, which are within thy gates,
shall come, and shall eat and be satisfied;
that the LORD thy God may bless thee in
all the work of thine hand which thou doest.

DEUTERONOMY 14:29

Then Jesus beholding him loved him, and said unto him,
One thing thou lackest: go thy way, sell whatsoever thou hast,
and give to the poor, and thou shalt have treasure in heaven:
and come, take up the cross, and follow me.

MARK 10:21

He is ever merciful, and lendeth;
and his seed is blessed.

PSALM 37:26

Like a mighty army moves the Church of God;
Brothers, we are treading where the saints have trod.
We are not divided, all one body we,
One in hope and doctrine, one in charity.

"ONWARD, CHRISTIAN SOLDIERS," SABINE BARING-GOULD

CHILDREN

＊ ・ ＊

Dear Lord, the children You have placed
in my life are such blessings. Help me
to be an example of Your love and patience,
to lead them closer to You, no matter
the circumstance. Amen.

And they said, Believe on the Lord Jesus Christ,
and thou shalt be saved, and thy house.
Acts 16:31

For the promise is unto you, and to your children,
and to all that are afar off, even as many as the
Lord our God shall call.
Acts 2:39

And all thy children shall be taught of the Lord;
and great shall be the peace of thy children.
Isaiah 54:13

For I will pour water upon him that is thirsty,
and floods upon the dry ground: I will pour my spirit
upon thy seed, and my blessing upon thine offspring.
Isaiah 44:3

Bring in the children, O bring them today;
Speak to them gently, and show them the way;
Careless they wander, and thoughtless they roam;
Bring in the children, for here is their home.

"Bring In the Children," Fanny Crosby

Thy wife shall be as a fruitful vine
by the sides of thine house:
thy children like olive plants
round about thy table.
Psalm 128:3

Lo, children are an heritage of the Lord:
and the fruit of the womb is his reward.
As arrows are in the hand of a mighty man;
so are children of the youth.
Happy is the man that hath his quiver full of them:
they shall not be ashamed, but they shall
speak with the enemies in the gate.
Psalm 127:3–5

Yet setteth he the poor on high from affliction,
and maketh him families like a flock.
Psalm 107:41

Children's children are the crown of old men;
and the glory of children are their fathers.

Precious blessings we receive,
When on Jesus we believe,
And are walking in the Spirit day by day;
When His Word is our delight,
And our path is growing bright,
While by faith we learn to trust
Him and obey.

"PRECIOUS BLESSINGS," FANNY CROSBY

....
....
....
....
....
....
....
....
....
....
....
....
....

CHILDREN'S DUTIES

Dear God, help me to be an example of obedience to my children. I pray that they would see me modeling obedience to You through my words and actions. May they follow in my footsteps, Lord. Amen.

Children, obey your parents in
the Lord: for this is right.
Honour thy father and mother;
which is the first commandment with promise;
that it may be well with thee, and thou
mayest live long on the earth.
EPHESIANS 6:1–3

Children, obey your parents in all things:
for this is well pleasing unto the Lord.
COLOSSIANS 3:20

Honour thy father and thy mother.
LUKE 18:20

Cursed be he that setteth light
by his father or his mother.
DEUTERONOMY 27:16

Ye shall fear every man his mother, and his father.
LEVITICUS 19:3

Honour thy father and thy mother,
as the LORD thy God hath commanded thee.
DEUTERONOMY 5:16

My son, keep thy father's commandment,
and forsake not the law of thy mother.
PROVERBS 6:20

A wise son heareth his father's instruction:
but a scorner heareth not rebuke.
PROVERBS 13:1

Let little children come to Me,
So says our blessèd Lord;
And I, a little child, must be
Obedient to His Word;
On Sabbath days must sing His praise,
And bow before Him, for He says,
Let little children come to Me,
Let little children come.

"LET LITTLE CHILDREN COME TO ME," JAMES REED

My son, if sinners entice thee, consent thou not.
PROVERBS 1:10

A fool despiseth his father's instruction:
but he that regardeth reproof is prudent.
PROVERBS 15:5

Even a child is known by his doings,
whether his work be pure, and whether it be right.
PROVERBS 20:11

A wise son maketh a glad father:
but a foolish son is the heaviness of his mother.
PROVERBS 10:1

Whoso keepeth the law is a wise son:
but he that is a companion of riotous men shameth his father.
PROVERBS 28:7

Now therefore hearken unto me, O ye children:
for blessed are they that keep my ways.
Hear instruction, and be wise, and refuse it not.
PROVERBS 8:32–33

My son, if thine heart be wise, my heart shall rejoice,
even mine. Yea, my reins shall rejoice,
when thy lips speak right things.
PROVERBS 23:15–16

Hearken unto thy father that begat thee,
and despise not thy mother when she is old.

PROVERBS 23:22

The father of the righteous shall greatly rejoice:
and he that begetteth a wise child shall have joy of him.
Thy father and thy mother shall be glad,
and she that bare thee shall rejoice.
My son, give me thine heart,
and let thine eyes observe my ways.

PROVERBS 23:24–26

Our Father, Thou in Heav'n above,
Who biddest us to dwell in love,
As brethren of one family,
To cry in every need to Thee,
Teach us no thoughtless words to say,
But from our inmost heart to pray.

"OUR FATHER, THOU IN HEAV'N ABOVE," MARTIN LUTHER

....

....

....

....

....

....

....

....

COMFORT

*Lord, I find myself turning to people and
things for comfort when I am discouraged.
Help me to realize that no one and no
thing will provide the lasting comfort that
I crave—that is, except You, Father. Amen.*

God is our refuge and strength, a very present help in trouble.
Therefore will not we fear, though the earth be removed,
and though the mountains be carried into the midst of the sea;
though the waters thereof roar and be troubled,
though the mountains shake with the swelling thereof.
PSALM 46:1–3

Though I walk in the midst of trouble,
thou wilt revive me:
thou shalt stretch forth thine hand
against the wrath of mine enemies,
and thy right hand shall save me.
PSALM 138:7

The LORD is my rock, and my fortress, and my deliverer;
my God, my strength, in whom I will trust; my buckler,
and the horn of my salvation, and my high tower.
PSALM 18:2

For he hath not despised nor
abhorred the affliction of the afflicted;
neither hath he hid his face from him;
but when he cried unto him, he heard.

PSALM 22:24

Though he fall, he shall not be utterly cast down:
for the LORD upholdeth him with his hand.

PSALM 37:24

The LORD is good, a strong hold in the day of trouble;
and he knoweth them that trust in him.

NAHUM 1:7

But the salvation of the righteous is of the LORD:
he is their strength in the time of trouble.

PSALM 37:39

God of all comfort, calm and fair
Stretch the broad plains beneath Thine eye;
And silent, through the hazy air,
Rise the blue hills to meet the sky.
The music of the Sabbath bells
Floats softly on the balmy air,
And the green earth in thousand tones
Lifts to Thy throne her grateful prayer.

"GOD OF ALL COMFORT," EMILY MILLER

Cast thy burden upon the LORD,
and he shall sustain thee:
he shall never suffer the righteous to be moved.
PSALM 55:22

These things I have spoken unto you,
that in me ye might have peace.
In the world ye shall have tribulation:
but be of good cheer; I have overcome the world.
JOHN 16:33

Come unto me, all ye that labour and
are heavy laden, and I will give you rest.
MATTHEW 11:28

For as the sufferings of Christ abound in us,
so our consolation also aboundeth by Christ.
2 CORINTHIANS 1:5

The LORD also will be a refuge for the oppressed,
a refuge in times of trouble.
PSALM 9:9

For the LORD will not cast off for ever:
but though he cause grief,
yet will he have compassion according
to the multitude of his mercies.
For he doth not afflict willingly nor
grieve the children of men.
LAMENTATIONS 3:31–33

Wait on the LORD: be of good courage,
and he shall strengthen thine heart:
wait, I say, on the LORD.
PSALM 27:14

O comfort to the dreary!
O joy to the oppressed!
Come unto Me, ye weary,
And I will give you rest.
O come in all your weakness!
Ye sons of guilt and woe;
And learn of Him with meekness,
Who stooped for us so low.

"O COMFORT TO THE DREARY," JOSIAH CONDER

CONTENTMENT

‡————— • —————‡

Lord, it's so easy for me to look around at what
my friends and family have and be envious.
Please help me to find contentment with what
I have and to be thankful for everything
You have given me. Amen.

A merry heart doeth good like a medicine:
but a broken spirit drieth the bones.
PROVERBS 17:22

Let your conversation be without covetousness;
and be content with such things as ye have:
for he hath said, I will never leave thee, nor forsake thee.
HEBREWS 13:5

All the days of the afflicted are evil:
but he that is of a merry heart hath a continual feast.

PROVERBS 15:15

A sound heart is the life of the flesh:
but envy the rottenness of the bones.
PROVERBS 14:30

But godliness with contentment is great gain.
1 TIMOTHY 6:6

Let not thine heart envy sinners: but be thou
in the fear of the LORD all the day long.
For surely there is an end; and thine
expectation shall not be cut off.
PROVERBS 23:17–18

Would you walk with the Lord,
In the light of His Word,
And have peace and contentment alway?
You must do His sweet will,
To be free from all ill,
On the altar your all you must lay.

"IS YOUR ALL ON THE ALTAR?" ELISHA A. HOFFMAN

CORRECTION, GOD'S

Dear Lord, I know that I am sometimes in need of correction. When my path goes astray and I am not walking in Your will, please correct me and bring me safely back to Your side. Amen.

For whom the LORD loveth he correcteth;
even as a father the son in whom he delighteth.
PROVERBS 3:12

Thou shalt also consider in thine heart,
that, as a man chasteneth his son,
so the LORD thy God chasteneth thee.
Therefore thou shalt keep the commandments
of the LORD thy God, to walk in his ways, and to fear him.
DEUTERONOMY 8:5–6

Blessed is the man whom thou chastenest,
O LORD, and teachest him out of thy law;
that thou mayest give him rest from the days of
adversity, until the pit be digged for the wicked.
PSALM 94:12–13

Door of my heart, I hasten!
Thee will I open wide.
Though He rebuke and chasten,
He shall with me abide.

"WHO AT MY DOOR IS STANDING?" MARY B. SLADE

For which cause we faint not;
but though our outward man perish,
yet the inward man is renewed day by day.
For our light affliction, which is but for a moment,
worketh for us a far more exceeding
and eternal weight of glory.
2 CORINTHIANS 4:16–17

For whom the Lord loveth he chasteneth,
and scourgeth every son whom he receiveth.
If ye endure chastening, God dealeth with you as with sons;
for what son is he whom the father chasteneth not?
HEBREWS 12:6–7

But when we are judged, we are chastened
of the Lord, that we should not be
condemned with the world.
1 CORINTHIANS 11:32

The Word by inspiration giv'n,
The chart that points the way to Heav'n;
On this I dare and will depend,
And with my life its truth defend.

"A Bible Christian," A. M. K. Diedrick

COURAGE

Dear God, fear is such a constant in this life. Give me the courage to overcome all my doubts and fears. Continue to show me that true courage is not a feeling but a daily action. Amen.

Wait on the LORD: be of good courage,
and he shall strengthen thine heart:
wait, I say, on the LORD.
PSALM 27:14

For the LORD loveth judgment,
and forsaketh not his saints;
they are preserved for ever: but the
seed of the wicked shall be cut off.
PSALM 37:28

But now thus saith the LORD that
created thee, O Jacob, and he that
formed thee, O Israel, Fear not:
for I have redeemed thee, I have called
thee by thy name; thou art mine.
ISAIAH 43:1

Fear not: for they that be with us
are more than they that be with them.
2 KINGS 6:16

With courage strong, we'll march along,
Christ's banner ever floating o'er us;
With purpose true His will to do
We'll vanquish every foe before us.

"WITH COURAGE STRONG," BELL HARRINGTON

Trust in the LORD, and do good;
so shalt thou dwell in the land,
and verily thou shalt be fed.
PSALM 37:3

He giveth power to the faint;
and to them that have no
might he increaseth strength.
ISAIAH 40:29

Be of good courage, and he shall
strengthen your heart,
all ye that hope in the LORD.
PSALM 31:24

I know both how to be abased, and I know how
to abound: every where and in all things I am
instructed both to be full and to be hungry,
both to abound and to suffer need. I can do
all things through Christ which strengtheneth me.
PHILIPPIANS 4:12–13

Press onward, press onward, your courage renew;
The prize is before you, the crown is in view;
His love is so boundless, He'll never say nay
To those who confess Him, believe, and obey.

"BELIEVE AND OBEY," FANNY CROSBY

DEATH

—•—

Heavenly Father, I know that death is a part of life, but that does not mean I am not afraid of it. Remind me that You are more powerful than anything in this world, even death. Amen.

Yea, though I walk through the valley of
the shadow of death, I will fear no evil:
for thou art with me; thy rod and
thy staff they comfort me.
PSALM 23:4

O death, where is thy sting?
O grave, where is thy victory?
1 CORINTHIANS 15:55

The wicked is driven away in his wickedness:
but the righteous hath hope in his death.
PROVERBS 14:32

Much more then, being now justified by his blood,
we shall be saved from wrath through him.
ROMANS 5:9

Verily, verily, I say unto you,
If a man keep my saying, he shall never see death.

JOHN 8:51

For this God is our God for ever and ever:
he will be our guide even unto death.

PSALM 48:14

But God will redeem my soul from the
power of the grave: for he shall receive me.

PSALM 49:15

It is not death to die,
To leave this weary road,
And midst the brotherhood on high
To be at home with God.
It is not death to close
The eye long dimmed by tears,
And wake, in glorious repose,
To spend eternal years.

"IT IS NOT DEATH TO DIE," H. A. CÉSAR MALAN

My flesh and my heart faileth: but God is the
strength of my heart, and my portion for ever.

PSALM 73:26

He will swallow up death in victory; and the
Lord GOD will wipe away tears from off all faces.

ISAIAH 25:8

I will ransom them from the power of the grave;
I will redeem them from death: O death, I will be
thy plagues; O grave, I will be thy destruction:
repentance shall be hid from mine eyes.
HOSEA 13:14

Precious in the sight of the LORD is the death of his saints.
PSALM 116:15

Mark the perfect man, and behold the
upright: for the end of that man is peace.
PSALM 37:37

But though our outward man perish,
yet the inward man is renewed day by day.
2 CORINTHIANS 4:16

That whosoever believeth in him
should not perish, but have eternal life.
JOHN 3:15

For I am persuaded, that neither death, nor life, nor angels,
nor principalities, nor powers, nor things present, nor things
to come, nor height, nor depth, nor any other creature,
shall be able to separate us from the love of God,
which is in Christ Jesus our Lord.
ROMANS 8:38–39

In one true God we all believe,
And to His name all glory give,
Creator of all things is He
In the Heav'n, the earth, the sea.

"In One True God We All Believe," Juraj Tranovský

....

....

....

....

....

....

....

....

....

....

....

....

....

....

....

....

ENEMIES

When I encounter people I disagree with or who are openly antagonistic, please help me to have patience and to find a way to love them, Lord. You are such a perfect example of loving Your enemies. Thank You, Father. Amen.

And the LORD shall help them, and deliver them:
he shall deliver them from the wicked,
and save them, because they trust in him.
PSALM 37:40

The LORD hath sworn by his right hand, and by the arm
of his strength, Surely I will no more give thy corn to be
meat for thine enemies; and the sons of the stranger shall
not drink thy wine, for the which thou hast laboured.
ISAIAH 62:8

For the rod of the wicked shall not rest upon the lot of the
righteous; lest the righteous put forth their hands unto iniquity.
PSALM 125:3

His heart is established, he shall not be afraid,
until he see his desire upon his enemies.
PSALM 112:8

Thy right hand, O LORD, is become glorious in power:
thy right hand, O LORD, hath dashed in pieces the enemy.
EXODUS 15:6

Through God we shall do valiantly:
for he it is that shall tread down our enemies.
PSALM 60:12

No weapon that is formed against thee shall prosper;
and every tongue that shall rise against thee in judgment
thou shalt condemn. This is the heritage of the servants of
the LORD, and their righteousness is of me, saith the LORD.
ISAIAH 54:17

When a man's ways please the LORD,
he maketh even his enemies to be at peace with him.
PROVERBS 16:7

The LORD taketh my part with them that help me:
therefore shall I see my desire upon them that hate me.
PSALM 118:7

That he would grant unto us, that we being delivered
out of the hand of our enemies might serve him without fear.
LUKE 1:74

The LORD shall cause thine enemies that rise up against
thee to be smitten before thy face: they shall come out
against thee one way, and flee before thee seven ways.
DEUTERONOMY 28:7

O God, my strength, on Thee I wait,
To Thee for refuge flee;
My God with mercy will defend,
Triumphant I shall be.

"PROTECT AND SAVE ME, O MY GOD," FROM *THE PSALTER*

For the LORD your God is he that goeth with you,
to fight for you against your enemies, to save you.
DEUTERONOMY 20:4

And shall not God avenge his own elect, which cry day and
night unto him, though he bear long with them?
LUKE 18:7

Behold, they shall surely gather together,
but not by me: whosoever shall gather together
against thee shall fall for thy sake.
ISAIAH 54:15

But I will deliver thee in that day, saith the LORD: and thou
shalt not be given into the hand of the men of whom thou
art afraid. For I will surely deliver thee, and thou shalt not
fall by the sword, but thy life shall be for a prey unto thee:
because thou hast put thy trust in me, saith the LORD.
JEREMIAH 39:17–18

Ye that love the LORD, hate evil: he preserveth the souls of his saints; he delivereth them out of the hand of the wicked.
PSALM 97:10

But the LORD your God ye shall fear; and he shall deliver you out of the hand of all your enemies.
2 KINGS 17:39

And he answered, Fear not: for they that be with us are more than they that be with them.
2 KINGS 6:16

Be not afraid of sudden fear, neither of the desolation of the wicked, when it cometh. For the LORD shall be thy confidence, and shall keep thy foot from being taken.
PROVERBS 3:25–26

That we should be saved from our enemies, and from the hand of all that hate us.
LUKE 1:71

For I am with thee, and no man shall set on thee to hurt thee: for I have much people in this city.
ACTS 18:10

So that we may boldly say, The Lord is my helper, and I will not fear what man shall do unto me.
HEBREWS 13:6

God is love; we're His little children.
God is love; we would be like Him.
'Tis love that makes us happy,
'Tis love that smoothes the way;
It helps us "mind," it makes us kind
To others every day.

"'TIS LOVE THAT MAKES US HAPPY," FRANKLIN E. BELDEN

ETERNAL LIFE

———◆ • ◆———

Lord, thank You for Your promise of eternal life.
Help me to focus on that promise when I become
overwhelmed with the tedious or stressful
moments of this life on earth. Amen.

Verily, verily, I say unto you,
He that believeth on me hath everlasting life.
JOHN 6:47

Jesus said unto her, I am the resurrection, and the life:
he that believeth in me, though he were dead, yet shall he live:
and whosoever liveth and believeth in me shall never die.
Believest thou this?
JOHN 11:25–26

And this is the promise that he
hath promised us, even eternal life.
1 JOHN 2:25

For the Lord himself shall descend from heaven with
a shout, with the voice of the archangel, and with the
trump of God: and the dead in Christ shall rise first.
1 THESSALONIANS 4:16

For since by man came death,
by man came also the resurrection of the dead.
1 Corinthians 15:21

These things have I written unto you that believe on the name
of the Son of God; that ye may know that ye have eternal life,
and that ye may believe on the name of the Son of God.
1 John 5:13

Marvel not at this: for the hour is coming,
in the which all that are in the graves shall hear his voice,
and shall come forth; they that have done good,
unto the resurrection of life; and they that have done evil,
unto the resurrection of damnation.
John 5:28–29

For God so loved the world, that he gave his only
begotten Son, that whosoever believeth in him
should not perish, but have everlasting life.
John 3:16

So also is the resurrection of the dead. It is sown in corruption;
it is raised in incorruption: it is sown in dishonour;
it is raised in glory: it is sown in weakness; it is raised in power:
It is sown a natural body; it is raised a spiritual body.
There is a natural body, and there is a spiritual body.
1 Corinthians 15:42–44

But if the Spirit of him that raised up Jesus from the dead dwell in you, he that raised up Christ from the dead shall also quicken your mortal bodies by his Spirit that dwelleth in you.

ROMANS 8:11

To him that in Thy name believes
Eternal life with Thee is given;
Into Himself He all receives,
Pardon and holiness, and Heaven.

"AUTHOR OF FAITH, ETERNAL WORD," CHARLES WESLEY

And God shall wipe away all tears from their eyes; and there shall be no more death, neither sorrow, nor crying, neither shall there be any more pain: for the former things are passed away.

REVELATION 21:4

And though after my skin worms destroy this body, yet in my flesh shall I see God: whom I shall see for myself, and mine eyes shall behold, and not another; though my reins be consumed within me.

JOB 19:26–27

For he that soweth to his flesh shall of the flesh reap corruption; but he that soweth to the Spirit shall of the Spirit reap life everlasting.

GALATIANS 6:8

For the wages of sin is death; but the gift of God
is eternal life through Jesus Christ our Lord.
ROMANS 6:23

For we know that if our earthly house of this tabernacle
were dissolved, we have a building of God, an house
not made with hands, eternal in the heavens.
2 CORINTHIANS 5:1

And many of them that sleep in the dust of the
earth shall awake, some to everlasting life,
and some to shame and everlasting contempt.
DANIEL 12:2

Thy dead men shall live, together with my dead body shall
they arise. Awake and sing, ye that dwell in dust: for thy dew
is as the dew of herbs, and the earth shall cast out the dead.
ISAIAH 26:19

For thou wilt not leave my soul in hell; neither wilt
thou suffer thine Holy One to see corruption.
PSALM 16:10

But is now made manifest by the appearing of our Saviour
Jesus Christ, who hath abolished death, and hath
brought life and immortality to light through the gospel.
2 TIMOTHY 1:10

And this is the record, that God hath given
to us eternal life, and this life is in his Son.
1 JOHN 5:11

In my Father's house are many mansions: if it were not so,
I would have told you. I go to prepare a place for you. And if I
go and prepare a place for you, I will come again, and receive
you unto myself; that where I am, there ye may be also.
JOHN 14:2-3

Everlasting life! is the promise giv'n unto them
Who love the Savior dear.
Everlasting life! and a home in Heav'n,
If you will believe His name.

"EVERLASTING LIFE," WILLIAM A. OGDEN

....
....
....
....
....
....
....
....
....
....
....

FAITH

✦————•————✦

Lord, I do not have perfect faith, but it is what I desire.
Continue to teach me to fully trust You with every
detail of my life and to have faith that You care and
have everything in the palm of Your hand. Amen.

Now faith is the substance of things hoped for,
the evidence of things not seen.
HEBREWS 11:1

Watch ye, stand fast in the faith,
quit you like men, be strong.
1 CORINTHIANS 16:13

If any of you lack wisdom, let him ask of God, that giveth to all
men liberally, and upbraideth not; and it shall be given him.
But let him ask in faith, nothing wavering. For he that wavereth
is like a wave of the sea driven with the wind and tossed.
JAMES 1:5–6

As ye have therefore received Christ Jesus the Lord,
so walk ye in him: rooted and built up in him,
and stablished in the faith, as ye have been
taught, abounding therein with thanksgiving.
COLOSSIANS 2:6–7

For by grace are ye saved through faith;
and that not of yourselves: it is the gift of God.
EPHESIANS 2:8

For ye are all the children
of God by faith in Christ Jesus.
GALATIANS 3:26

Faith of our fathers, living still,
In spite of dungeon, fire, and sword;
O how our hearts beat high with joy
Whenever we hear that glorious Word!
Faith of our fathers, holy faith!
We will be true to thee till death.

"FAITH OF OUR FATHERS," FREDERICK FABER

The fruit of the Spirit is love, joy, peace, longsuffering,
gentleness, goodness, faith, meekness, temperance:
against such there is no law.
GALATIANS 5:22–23

But continue thou in the things which thou hast learned
and hast been assured of, knowing of whom thou hast
learned them; and that from a child thou hast known the
holy scriptures, which are able to make thee wise unto
salvation through faith which is in Christ Jesus.
2 TIMOTHY 3:14–15

For we walk by faith, not by sight.
2 CORINTHIANS 5:7

And Jesus answering saith unto them, Have faith in God.
For verily I say unto you, That whosoever shall say unto this
mountain, Be thou removed, and be thou cast into the sea;
and shall not doubt in his heart, but shall believe that those things
which he saith shall come to pass; he shall have whatsoever he saith.
MARK 11:22–23

I am crucified with Christ: nevertheless I live;
yet not I, but Christ liveth in me: and the life which
I now live in the flesh I live by the faith of the Son
of God, who loved me, and gave himself for me.
GALATIANS 2:20

He that cometh to God must believe that he is,
and that he is a rewarder of them that
diligently seek him.
HEBREWS 11:6

Lord, I believe; but Thou dost know
My faith is cold and weak;
Pity my frailty, and bestow
The confidence I seek.

"LORD, I BELIEVE," JOHN R. WREFORD

FAITHFULNESS, GOD'S

-+-------·-------+-

Dear Lord, even though I often struggle in my daily walk with You, I know Your faithfulness is perfect. Thank You for never leaving me or forsaking me. Although I know I don't deserve it, I am continually grateful for Your faithfulness. Amen.

Know therefore that the LORD thy God, he is God, the faithful God, which keepeth covenant and mercy with them that love him and keep his commandments to a thousand generations.
DEUTERONOMY 7:9

(For the LORD thy God is a merciful God;) he will not forsake thee, neither destroy thee, nor forget the covenant of thy fathers which he sware unto them.
DEUTERONOMY 4:31

He hath remembered his covenant for ever, the word which he commanded to a thousand generations.
PSALM 105:8

God is not a man, that he should lie; neither the son of man, that he should repent: hath he said, and shall he not do it? or hath he spoken, and shall he not make it good?
NUMBERS 23:19

Let us hold fast the profession of our faith without
wavering; (for he is faithful that promised).
HEBREWS 10:23

If we believe not, yet he abideth faithful:
he cannot deny himself.
2 TIMOTHY 2:13

The Lord is not slack concerning his promise,
as some men count slackness; but is longsuffering to us-ward.
2 PETER 3:9

Blessed be the LORD, that hath given rest unto his people
Israel, according to all that he promised: there hath
not failed one word of all his good promise.
1 KINGS 8:56

In God, my faithful God,
I trust when dark my road;
Though many woes o'ertake me,
Yet He will not forsake me;
His love it is doth send them,
And when 'tis best will end them.

"IN GOD, MY FAITHFUL GOD," SIGISMUND WEINGÄRTNER

O Lord, thou art my God; I will exalt thee,
I will praise thy name; for thou hast done wonderful things;
thy counsels of old are faithfulness and truth.
ISAIAH 25:1

And they that know thy name will put their trust in thee:
for thou, LORD, hast not forsaken them that seek thee.
PSALM 9:10

My covenant will I not break, nor alter
the thing that is gone out of my lips.
PSALM 89:34

Thy faithfulness, Lord, each moment we find,
So true to Thy Word, so loving and kind!
Thy mercy so tender to all the lost race,
The vilest offender may turn and find grace.

"THY FAITHFULNESS, LORD, EACH MOMENT WE FIND," CHARLES WESLEY

FEAR

Heavenly Father, fear seems to have a constant grip on my mind and spirit; I want to be free of its hold on me. Please take away those fears that I can't seem to shake, and show me how to daily give them over to You. Amen.

And he said unto them, Why are ye so fearful?
how is it that ye have no faith?
MARK 4:40

Fear not, little flock; for it is your Father's
good pleasure to give you the kingdom.
LUKE 12:32

For I the LORD thy God will hold thy right hand,
saying unto thee, Fear not; I will help thee.
ISAIAH 41:13

But whoso hearkeneth unto me shall dwell safely,
and shall be quiet from fear of evil.
PROVERBS 1:33

And fear not them which kill the body,
but are not able to kill the soul.
MATTHEW 10:28

Be not afraid of sudden fear, neither of the desolation of
the wicked, when it cometh. For the LORD shall be thy
confidence, and shall keep thy foot from being taken.
PROVERBS 3:25–26

For God hath not given us the spirit of fear;
but of power, and of love, and of a sound mind.
2 TIMOTHY 1:7

The LORD shall give thee rest from thy sorrow,
and from thy fear, and from the hard bondage
wherein thou wast made to serve.
ISAIAH 14:3

When thou liest down, thou shalt not be afraid:
yea, thou shalt lie down, and thy sleep shall be sweet.
PROVERBS 3:24

In righteousness shalt thou be established:
thou shalt be far from oppression; for thou shalt not fear:
and from terror; for it shall not come near thee.
ISAIAH 54:14

I, even I, am he that comforteth you: who art thou,
that thou shouldest be afraid of a man that shall die,
and of the son of man which shall be made as grass.
ISAIAH 51:12

O love that casts out fear,
O love that casts out sin,
Tarry no more without,
But come and dwell within! . . .

Great love of God, come in!
Wellspring of heavenly peace;
Thou Living Water, come!
Spring up, and never cease.

"O LOVE THAT CASTS OUT FEAR," HORATIUS BONAR

For ye have not received the spirit of bondage again
to fear; but ye have received the Spirit of adoption,
whereby we cry, Abba, Father.
ROMANS 8:15

So that we may boldly say, The Lord is my helper,
and I will not fear what man shall do unto me.
HEBREWS 13:6

God is our refuge and strength,
a very present help in trouble.
PSALM 46:1

The fear of man bringeth a snare: but whoso
putteth his trust in the LORD shall be safe.
PROVERBS 29:25

Fear not; for thou shalt not be ashamed:
neither be thou confounded.

ISAIAH 54:4

When thou passest through the waters, I will be with thee;
and through the rivers, they shall not overflow thee:
when thou walkest through the fire, thou shalt not be burned;
neither shall the flame kindle upon thee.

ISAIAH 43:2

Peace I leave with you, my peace I give unto you:
not as the world giveth, give I unto you. Let not
your heart be troubled, neither let it be afraid.

JOHN 14:27

Simply to His grace and wholly
Light and life and strength belong,
And I love supremely, solely,
Him the holy, Him the strong.

"FIRMLY I BELIEVE AND TRULY," JOHN H. NEWMAN

....

....

....

....

....

....

....

FOOD AND CLOTHING

------❖------•------❖------

God, You have provided for me in every material way. You give me the things that I need, and for that I am so incredibly thankful. I will continue to trust Your provision and rely on Your unfailing generosity. Amen.

He maketh peace in thy borders,
and filleth thee with the finest of the wheat.
PSALM 147:14

He hath given meat unto them that fear him:
he will ever be mindful of his covenant.
PSALM 111:5

We thank You, Lord, for everyday provisions,
For daily food, for clothes and shelter too,
For health and strength and grace for every trial,
For this free land where we can worship You.
You crown each day with Your abundant goodness;
We thank You, Lord, and lift our praise to You.

"WE THANK YOU, LORD," SUSAN H. PETERSON

And ye shall eat in plenty, and be satisfied, and praise the name of the LORD your God, that hath dealt wondrously with you: and my people shall never be ashamed.

JOEL 2:26

Therefore take no thought, saying, What shall we eat? or, What shall we drink? or, Wherewithal shall we be clothed? (For after all these things do the Gentiles seek:) for your heavenly Father knoweth that ye have need of all these things.

MATTHEW 6:31–32

Great is Thy faithfulness!
Great is Thy faithfulness!
Morning by morning new mercies I see.
All I have needed Thy hand hath provided;
Great is Thy faithfulness, Lord, unto me!

"GREAT IS THY FAITHFULNESS," THOMAS O. CHISHOLM

FORGIVENESS

Dear God, thank You for being the perfect example of forgiveness. I struggle to forgive those I love and those I don't get along with. You forgave people who openly hated You and put You to death on a cross. Help me to remember Your example when I'm struggling with forgiveness, Lord. Amen.

And when ye stand praying, forgive, if ye have ought against any: that your Father also which is in heaven may forgive you your trespasses. But if ye do not forgive, neither will your Father which is in heaven forgive your trespasses.
MARK 11:25–26

There is gladness in my heart today, today,
A peace I cannot tell,
For the Spirit of the Lord now dwells within,
And with my soul 'tis well.
There is gladness in my heart today,
Which peace and joy impart,
For the Spirit of the Lord has come to stay,
There's gladness in my heart.

"JOY OF FORGIVENESS," A. S. DEYOE

For if ye forgive men their trespasses,
your heavenly Father will also forgive you.

MATTHEW 6:14

Therefore if thine enemy hunger, feed him;
if he thirst, give him drink.

ROMANS 12:20

Praise the Father, who from Heaven
Unto us such food hath given
And, to mend what we have done,
Gave into death His only Son.

"PRAISE, MY SOUL, THE KING OF HEAVEN," HENRY F. LYTE

FRUITFULNESS

‑‑‑‑‑‑•‑‑‑‑‑‑

Lord, I was created to glorify You with every thought, word, and deed. It's so easy for me to lose sight of that when I get stressed and busy. Remind me that I need to be rooted in You and bear fruit for Your glory. Amen.

I am the true vine, and my Father is the husbandman. Every branch in me that beareth not fruit he taketh away: and every branch that beareth fruit, he purgeth it, that it may bring forth more fruit. Now ye are clean through the word which I have spoken unto you. Abide in me, and I in you. As the branch cannot bear fruit of itself, except it abide in the vine; no more can ye, except ye abide in me. I am the vine, ye are the branches: He that abideth in me, and I in him, the same bringeth forth much fruit: for without me ye can do nothing.
JOHN 15:1–5

And he shall be like a tree planted by the rivers of water, that bringeth forth his fruit in his season; his leaf also shall not wither; and whatsoever he doeth shall prosper.
PSALM 1:3

Sing to the Lord of harvest,
Sing songs of love and praise;
With joyful hearts and voices
Your alleluias raise.
By Him the rolling seasons
In fruitful order move;
Sing to the Lord of harvest,
A joyous song of love.

"SING TO THE LORD OF HARVEST," JOHN S. B. MONSELL

Therefore they shall come and sing in the height of Zion,
and shall flow together to the goodness of the LORD,
for wheat, and for wine, and for oil, and for the young of the
flock and of the herd: and their soul shall be as a watered
garden; and they shall not sorrow any more at all.
JEREMIAH 31:12

They shall still bring forth fruit in old age;
they shall be fat and flourishing.
PSALM 92:14

I will be as the dew unto Israel: he shall grow
as the lily, and cast forth his roots as Lebanon.
HOSEA 14:5

For if these things be in you, and abound,
they make you that ye shall neither be barren nor
unfruitful in the knowledge of our Lord Jesus Christ.
2 PETER 1:8

Happy is he that fears the Lord,
And follows His commands;
Who lends the poor without rewards,
Or gives with liberal hands.

"HAPPY IS HE THAT FEARS THE LORD," ISAAC WATTS

GOSSIP

✦━━━━━•━━━━━✦

*Heavenly Father, it's so easy for me to criticize
and say cruel or petty things behind others' backs.
Help me to think before I speak and wisely choose
the words that I use when speaking of others.*

Thou shalt not go up and down as a talebearer
among thy people: neither shalt thou stand against
the blood of thy neighbour; I am the LORD.
LEVITICUS 19:16

The words of a talebearer are as wounds,
and they go down into the innermost parts of the belly.
PROVERBS 18:8

He that goeth about as a talebearer revealeth secrets:
therefore meddle not with him that flattereth with his lips.
PROVERBS 20:19

A talebearer revealeth secrets:
but he that is of a faithful spirit concealeth the matter.
PROVERBS 11:13

Let every tongue Thy goodness speak,
Thou sovereign Lord of all;
Thy strengthening hands uphold the weak,
And raise the poor that fall.

"LET EVERY TONGUE THY GOODNESS SPEAK," ISAAC WATTS

A froward man soweth strife:
and a whisperer separateth chief friends.
PROVERBS 16:28

The tongue deviseth mischiefs;
like a sharp razor, working deceitfully.
PSALM 52:2

Where no wood is, there the fire goeth out: so where there
is no talebearer, the strife ceaseth. As coals are to burning
coals, and wood to fire; so is a contentious man to kindle
strife. The words of a talebearer are as wounds, and they
go down into the innermost parts of the belly.
PROVERBS 26:20–22

The north wind driveth away rain: so doth
an angry countenance a backbiting tongue.
PROVERBS 25:23

Keep thy tongue from evil,
and thy lips from speaking guile.
PSALM 34:13

All things are possible to him
That can in Jesus' name believe:
Lord, I no more Thy truth blaspheme,
Thy truth I lovingly receive;
I can, I do believe in Thee,
All things are possible to me.

"ALL THINGS ARE POSSIBLE," CHARLES WESLEY

....
....
....
....
....
....
....
....
....
....
....
....
....
....
....
....
....
....

GRACE, GROWTH IN

———•———

Dear Lord, I want to grow in You every day. When I am struggling with a lack of grace toward others or toward myself, replenish me with all of the grace that I need to get through the day. Amen.

Herein is my Father glorified, that ye bear
much fruit; so shall ye be my disciples.
JOHN 15:8

And this I pray, that your love may abound yet
more and more in knowledge and in all judgment.
PHILIPPIANS 1:9

Being filled with the fruits of righteousness, which are
by Jesus Christ, unto the glory and praise of God.
PHILIPPIANS 1:11

But we all, with open face beholding as in a glass the
glory of the Lord, are changed into the same image
from glory to glory, even as by the Spirit of the Lord.
2 CORINTHIANS 3:18

The LORD will perfect that which concerneth me:
thy mercy, O LORD, endureth for ever:
forsake not the works of thine own hands.
PSALM 138:8

But the path of the just is as the shining light,
that shineth more and more unto the perfect day.
PROVERBS 4:18

Amazing grace! How sweet the sound
That saved a wretch like me!
I once was lost, but now am found;
Was blind, but now I see.

"AMAZING GRACE," JOHN NEWTON

Which is come unto you, as it is in all the world;
and bringeth forth fruit, as it doth also in you, since the day
ye heard of it, and knew the grace of God in truth.
COLOSSIANS 1:6

I press toward the mark for the prize of the high calling of God
in Christ Jesus. Let us therefore, as many as be perfect, be thus
minded: and if in any thing ye be otherwise minded, God shall
reveal even this unto you. Nevertheless, whereto we have already
attained, let us walk by the same rule, let us mind the same thing.
PHILIPPIANS 3:14–16

Furthermore then we beseech you, brethren, and exhort you by the Lord Jesus, that as ye have received of us how ye ought to walk and to please God, so ye would abound more and more.

1 THESSALONIANS 4:1

Turn your eyes upon Jesus,
Look full in His wonderful face,
And the things of earth will grow strangely dim
In the light of His glory and grace.

"TURN YOUR EYES UPON JESUS," HELEN H. LEMMEL

GUIDANCE

—✦———•———✦—

Dear Lord, I need Your daily guidance in my life.
Help me to be able to recognize the nudges and directions
You give me, and make my heart sensitive to Your will.
Help me to joyfully follow wherever You lead. Amen.

And thine ears shall hear a word behind thee, saying,
This is the way, walk ye in it, when ye turn to the right hand,
and when ye turn to the left.
ISAIAH 30:21

For this God is our God for ever and ever:
he will be our guide even unto death.
PSALM 48:14

A man's heart deviseth his way:
but the LORD directeth his steps.
PROVERBS 16:9

The steps of a good man are ordered by
the LORD: and he delighteth in his way.
PSALM 37:23

Shepherd, show me how to go
O'er the hillside steep,
How to gather, how to sow,
How to feed Thy sheep.
I will listen for Thy voice,
Lest my footsteps stray;
I will follow and rejoice
All the rugged way.

"SHEPHERD, SHOW ME HOW TO GO," MARY B. EDDY

For his God doth instruct him to
discretion, and doth teach him.
ISAIAH 28:26

The righteousness of the perfect shall direct his way:
but the wicked shall fall by his own wickedness.
PROVERBS 11:5

In all thy ways acknowledge him,
and he shall direct thy paths.
PROVERBS 3:6

And I will bring the blind by a way that they knew not;
I will lead them in paths that they have not known:
I will make darkness light before them, and crooked things
straight. These things will I do unto them, and not forsake them.
ISAIAH 42:16

I build on this foundation, that Jesus and His blood
Alone are my salvation, the true eternal good;
Without Him, all that pleases is valueless on earth:
The gifts I owe to Jesus alone my love are worth.

"If God Himself Be for Me," Paul Gerhardt

GUILT

-•-

*Lord, I am constantly weighed down by guilt...
for things I've done wrong, for all the ways I've let
those around me down, and for how easily I can be
unfaithful to You. Please take this guilt from me.
Help me to live a life of freedom in You. Amen.*

If we confess our sins, he is faithful and just to forgive
us our sins, and to cleanse us from all unrighteousness.
1 JOHN 1:9

Let the wicked forsake his way, and the unrighteous man his
thoughts: and let him return unto the LORD, and he will have
mercy upon him; and to our God, for he will abundantly pardon.
ISAIAH 55:7

For the LORD your God is gracious and merciful, and will
not turn away his face from you, if ye return unto him.
2 CHRONICLES 30:9

As far as the east is from the west, so far hath
he removed our transgressions from us.
PSALM 103:12

For if our heart condemn us, God is greater
than our heart, and knoweth all things.
1 JOHN 3:20

For I will be merciful to their unrighteousness,
and their sins and their iniquities will I remember no more.
HEBREWS 8:12

Laden with guilt, and full of fears,
I fly to Thee, my Lord,
And not a glimpse of hope appears
But in Thy written Word.

The volume of my Father's grace
Does all my griefs assuage;
Here I behold my Savior's face
Almost in every page.

"LADEN WITH GUILT, AND FULL OF FEARS," ISAAC WATTS

Therefore if any man be in Christ, he is a new creature:
old things are passed away; behold, all things are become new.
2 CORINTHIANS 5:17

For I will forgive their iniquity,
and I will remember their sin no more.
JEREMIAH 31:34

And I will cleanse them from all their iniquity,
whereby they have sinned against me; and I will pardon
all their iniquities, whereby they have sinned, and whereby
they have transgressed against me.

JEREMIAH 33:8

I, even I, am he that blotteth out thy transgressions
for mine own sake, and will not remember thy sins.

ISAIAH 43:25

Why not believe the glad good news?
Why still the voice of God refuse?
Why not believe, when God hath said,
All, all our guilt on Him was laid.

"HE THAT BELIEVETH," PHILIP P. BLISS

....
....
....
....
....
....
....
....
....
....
....

HELP IN TROUBLES

❦ • ❦

*Dear Lord, troubles will always come into my life, and
I need to consistently rely on You to help me through
them. Help me to remember that no matter how big or
small my troubles may be, You are there—and You
will never let me go through anything alone. Amen.*

But the salvation of the righteous is of the LORD:
he is their strength in the time of trouble.
PSALM 37:39

The LORD openeth the eyes of the blind:
the LORD raiseth them that are bowed down:
the LORD loveth the righteous.
PSALM 146:8

The LORD is good, a strong hold in the day of trouble;
and he knoweth them that trust in him.
NAHUM 1:7

Though he fall, he shall not be utterly cast down:
for the LORD upholdeth him with his hand.
PSALM 37:24

Thou art my hiding place; thou shalt preserve me from trouble;
thou shalt compass me about with songs of deliverance.
PSALM 32:7

Thou, which hast shewed me great and sore troubles,
shalt quicken me again, and shalt bring me up again
from the depths of the earth.
PSALM 71:20

Why art thou cast down, O my soul?
and why art thou disquieted within me?
hope thou in God: for I shall yet praise him,
who is the health of my countenance, and my God.
PSALM 42:11

My flesh and my heart faileth: but God is the
strength of my heart, and my portion for ever.
PSALM 73:26

There shall no evil befall thee, neither shall any plague
come nigh thy dwelling. For he shall give his angels
charge over thee, to keep thee in all thy ways.
PSALM 91:10–11

They that sow in tears shall reap in joy. He that goeth forth
and weepeth, bearing precious seed, shall doubtless come
again with rejoicing, bringing his sheaves with him.
PSALM 126:5–6

O love the LORD, all ye his saints: for the LORD preserveth
the faithful, and plentifully rewardeth the proud doer.
PSALM 31:23

Though troubles assail us and dangers affright,
Though friends should all fail us and foes all unite,
Yet one thing secures us, whatever betide,
The promise assures us, The Lord will provide.

"THOUGH TROUBLES ASSAIL US," JOHN NEWTON

Though ye have lien among the pots, yet shall ye
be as the wings of a dove covered with silver,
and her feathers with yellow gold.
PSALM 68:13

The LORD is my strength and my shield; my heart
trusted in him, and I am helped: therefore my heart
greatly rejoiceth; and with my song will I praise him.
PSALM 28:7

The LORD also will be a refuge for the
oppressed, a refuge in times of trouble.
PSALM 9:9

For he hath not despised nor abhorred the affliction of the
afflicted; neither hath he hid his face from him;
but when he cried unto him, he heard.
PSALM 22:24

Though I walk in the midst of trouble, thou wilt revive me:
thou shalt stretch forth thine hand against the wrath of
mine enemies, and thy right hand shall save me.

PSALM 138:7

Many are the afflictions of the righteous:
but the LORD delivereth him out of them all.

PSALM 34:19

For the LORD will not cast off for ever: but though
he cause grief, yet will he have compassion according
to the multitude of his mercies. For he doth not afflict
willingly nor grieve the children of men.

LAMENTATIONS 3:31–33

The LORD is my rock, and my fortress, and my deliverer;
my God, my strength, in whom I will trust; my buckler,
and the horn of my salvation, and my high tower.

PSALM 18:2

Rejoice not against me, O mine enemy: when I fall,
I shall arise; when I sit in darkness, the LORD shall be a
light unto me. I will bear the indignation of the LORD,
because I have sinned against him, until he plead my cause,
and execute judgment for me: he will bring me forth to
the light, and I shall behold his righteousness.

MICAH 7:8–9

These things I have spoken unto you, that in me ye might have peace. In the world ye shall have tribulation: but be of good cheer; I have overcome the world.

JOHN 16:33

His love in time past forbids me to think
He'll leave me at last in trouble to sink;
Each sweet Ebenezer I have in review,
Confirms His good pleasure to help me quite through.

"BEGONE, UNBELIEF," JOHN NEWTON

HOLY SPIRIT

Dear God, the Bible calls the Holy Spirit "the Great Comforter" and shares that He will abide with me forever. Help me to remember this beautiful promise when I am in need of comfort and feel all alone. Amen.

Behold, I will pour out my spirit unto you,
I will make known my words unto you.
PROVERBS 1:23

And I will pray the Father, and he shall give you another
Comforter, that he may abide with you for ever;
even the Spirit of truth; whom the world cannot receive,
because it seeth him not, neither knoweth him: but ye know
him; for he dwelleth with you, and shall be in you.
JOHN 14:16–17

He that believeth on me, as the scripture hath said,
out of his belly shall flow rivers of living water.
(But this spake he of the Spirit, which they that believe
on him should receive: for the Holy Ghost was not
yet given; because that Jesus was not yet glorified.)
JOHN 7:38–39

Howbeit when he, the Spirit of truth, is come, he will
guide you into all truth: for he shall not speak of himself;
but whatsoever he shall hear, that shall he speak:
and he will shew you things to come.

JOHN 16:13

If ye then, being evil, know how to give good gifts unto
your children: how much more shall your heavenly
Father give the Holy Spirit to them that ask him?

LUKE 11:13

Come, Holy Spirit, Dove divine,
On these baptismal waters shine,
And teach our hearts, in highest strain,
To praise the Lamb for sinners slain.

"COME, HOLY SPIRIT, DOVE DIVINE," ADONIRAM JUDSON

But whosoever drinketh of the water that I shall give him
shall never thirst; but the water that I shall give him shall
be in him a well of water springing up into everlasting life.

JOHN 4:14

And I will put my spirit within you, and cause
you to walk in my statutes, and ye shall
keep my judgments, and do them.

EZEKIEL 36:27

But the anointing which ye have received of him abideth in you, and ye need not that any man teach you: but as the same anointing teacheth you of all things, and is truth, and is no lie, and even as it hath taught you, ye shall abide in him.

1 JOHN 2:27

For ye have not received the spirit of bondage again to fear; but ye have received the Spirit of adoption, whereby we cry, Abba, Father.

ROMANS 8:15

Holy Spirit, truth divine,
Dawn upon this soul of mine;
Word of God and inward light,
Wake my spirit, clear my sight.

"HOLY SPIRIT, TRUTH DIVINE," SAMUEL LONGFELLOW

....
....
....
....
....
....
....
....
....
....

HONESTY

⸺⸱⸺

Dear Lord, I find it so hard to be honest sometimes. Being honest with others is difficult enough, but I sometimes struggle with being honest with myself about my own emotions and intentions. Help me to live honestly in every area of my life. Amen.

Ye shall not steal, neither deal falsely,
neither lie one to another.
LEVITICUS 19:11

Are there yet the treasures of wickedness in the house of the
wicked, and the scant measure that is abominable? Shall I
count them pure with the wicked balances, and with the bag
of deceitful weights? For the rich men thereof are full of
violence, and the inhabitants thereof have spoken lies,
and their tongue is deceitful in their mouth.
MICAH 6:10–12

Ye shall do no unrighteousness in judgment,
in meteyard, in weight, or in measure.
LEVITICUS 19:35

A false balance is abomination to the LORD:
but a just weight is his delight.
PROVERBS 11:1

But thou shalt have a perfect and just weight, a perfect
and just measure shalt thou have: that thy days may be
lengthened in the land which the LORD thy God giveth thee.
For all that do such things, and all that do unrighteously,
are an abomination unto the LORD thy God.
DEUTERONOMY 25:15-16

That no man go beyond and defraud his brother in any
matter: because that the Lord is the avenger of all such,
as we also have forewarned you and testified. For God
hath not called us unto uncleanness, but unto holiness.
1 THESSALONIANS 4:6-7

Lie not one to another, seeing that ye have put off the old man
with his deeds; and have put on the new man, which is renewed
in knowledge after the image of him that created him.
COLOSSIANS 3:9-10

May we receive the Word we hear,
Each in an honest heart,
And keep the precious treasure there,
And never with it part!

"ONCE MORE WE COME BEFORE OUR GOD," JOSEPH HART

The wicked borroweth, and payeth not again:
but the righteous sheweth mercy, and giveth.
Psalm 37:21

Withhold not good from them to whom it is due,
when it is in the power of thine hand to do it.
Proverbs 3:27

And if thou sell ought unto thy neighbour,
or buyest ought of thy neighbour's hand,
ye shall not oppress one another.
Leviticus 25:14

Ye shall not therefore oppress one another;
but thou shalt fear thy God: for I am the Lord your God.
Leviticus 25:17

Better is a little with righteousness
than great revenues without right.
Proverbs 16:8

He that walketh righteously, and speaketh uprightly; he that
despiseth the gain of oppressions, that shaketh his hands
from holding of bribes, that stoppeth his ears from hearing of
blood, and shutteth his eyes from seeing evil; he shall dwell
on high: his place of defence shall be the munitions of rocks:
bread shall be given him; his waters shall be sure.
Isaiah 33:15–16

I hear it so often, wherever I go,
That same old story was told;
And I've thought it was strange that so often they'd tell
That story as if it were new;
But I've found out the reason they loved it so well,
That old, old story is true.

"THAT OLD, OLD STORY IS TRUE," D. B. WATKINS

HOPE

—◆———•———◆—

*Dear Lord, Thank You for the eternal hope that
You have given me. . .the promise that this life is not
all that You have in store for me. Thank You for
providing for me now—and for all eternity. Help
me to never lose sight of Your provision. Amen.*

Why art thou cast down, O my soul?
and why art thou disquieted within me?
hope thou in God: for I shall yet praise him,
who is the health of my countenance, and my God.
PSALM 42:11

Who by him do believe in God, that raised
him up from the dead, and gave him glory;
that your faith and hope might be in God.
1 PETER 1:21

Wherefore gird up the loins of your mind, be sober,
and hope to the end for the grace that is to be brought
unto you at the revelation of Jesus Christ.
1 PETER 1:13

And every man that hath this hope in
him purifieth himself, even as he is pure.
1 JOHN 3:3

The wicked is driven away in his wickedness:
but the righteous hath hope in his death.
PROVERBS 14:32

———————————

All my hope on God is founded;
He doth still my trust renew,
Me through change and chance He guideth,
Only good and only true.
God unknown, He alone
Calls my heart to be His own.

"ALL MY HOPE ON GOD IS FOUNDED," JOACHIM NEANDER

———————————

For the hope which is laid up for you in heaven,
whereof ye heard before in the word of the truth of the gospel.
COLOSSIANS 1:5

Which is Christ in you, the hope of glory.
COLOSSIANS 1:27

Be of good courage, and he shall strengthen
your heart, all ye that hope in the LORD.
PSALM 31:24

For thou art my hope, O Lord GOD:
thou art my trust from my youth.
PSALM 71:5

Blessed be the God and Father of our Lord Jesus Christ,
which according to his abundant mercy hath begotten
us again unto a lively hope by the resurrection of
Jesus Christ from the dead.
1 PETER 1:3

Lay hold on the hope set before you,
And let not a moment be lost,
The Savior has purchased your ransom,
But think what a price it hath cost!

"THE HOPE SET BEFORE YOU," FANNY CROSBY

HOSPITALITY

Heavenly Father, I want to welcome others into my home and make them feel loved and appreciated. You are a perfect example of welcoming others. Help me to do the same and not worry about the state of my house but rather the joy of others' company. Amen.

Use hospitality one to another without grudging. As every man hath received the gift, even so minister the same one to another, as good stewards of the manifold grace of God.
1 PETER 4:9–10

If a brother or sister be naked, and destitute of daily food, and one of you say unto them, Depart in peace, be ye warmed and filled; notwithstanding ye give them not those things which are needful to the body; what doth it profit?
JAMES 2:15–16

For whosoever shall give you a cup of water to drink in my name, because ye belong to Christ, verily I say unto you, he shall not lose his reward.
MARK 9:41

I have shewed you all things, how that so labouring ye ought to support the weak, and to remember the words of the Lord Jesus, how he said, It is more blessed to give than to receive.

ACTS 20:35

But whoso hath this world's good, and seeth his brother have need, and shutteth up his bowels of compassion from him, how dwelleth the love of God in him?

1 JOHN 3:17

We would join in the song of welcome:
Welcome one and all today!
Let us strive with our might e'er to do the right,
And to seek for the lambs astray.

"WELCOME, ONE AND ALL," LAURA E. NEWELL

And the King shall answer and say unto them,
Verily I say unto you, Inasmuch as ye have done
it unto one of the least of these my brethren,
ye have done it unto me.

MATTHEW 25:40

Be not forgetful to entertain strangers:
for thereby some have entertained angels unawares.

HEBREWS 13:2

For I mean not that other men be eased, and ye burdened: but by an equality, that now at this time your abundance may be a supply for their want, that their abundance also may be a supply for your want: that there may be equality.

2 CORINTHIANS 8:13–14

Distributing to the necessity of saints; given to hospitality.

ROMANS 12:13

For I was an hungred, and ye gave me meat: I was thirsty, and ye gave me drink: I was a stranger, and ye took me in: naked, and ye clothed me: I was sick, and ye visited me: I was in prison, and ye came unto me.

MATTHEW 25:35–36

Still out of Christ, yet for you there is mercy,
If you are willing to turn from your sin;
Yonder He stands at the door of salvation,
Waiting to pardon and welcome you in.

"STILL OUT OF CHRIST," FANNY CROSBY

HUMILITY

Lord, humble me. Keep me from taking pride in my own accomplishments and abilities; in its place, let me point all praise toward You and lift up Your name in honor. Help me not to compare myself to others but to focus on serving them instead. Amen.

Whosoever therefore shall humble himself as this little child, the same is greatest in the kingdom of heaven.
MATTHEW 18:4

Lord, thou hast heard the desire of the humble: thou wilt prepare their heart, thou wilt cause thine ear to hear.
PSALM 10:17

And whosoever shall exalt himself shall be abased; and he that shall humble himself shall be exalted.
MATTHEW 23:12

For thus saith the high and lofty One that inhabiteth eternity, whose name is Holy; I dwell in the high and holy place, with him also that is of a contrite and humble spirit, to revive the spirit of the humble, and to revive the heart of the contrite ones.
ISAIAH 57:15

Better it is to be of an humble spirit with the lowly,
than to divide the spoil with the proud.
PROVERBS 16:19

But he giveth more grace. Wherefore he saith,
God resisteth the proud, but giveth grace unto the humble.
JAMES 4:6

Blest are the humble souls that see
Their emptiness and poverty;
Treasures of grace to them are giv'n,
And crowns of joy laid up in Heav'n.

"BLEST ARE THE HUMBLE SOULS THAT SEE," ISAAC WATTS

When he maketh inquisition for blood, he remembereth
them: he forgetteth not the cry of the humble.
PSALM 9:12

By humility and the fear of the LORD
are riches, and honour, and life.
PROVERBS 22:4

Surely he scorneth the scorners:
but he giveth grace unto the lowly.
PROVERBS 3:34

The fear of the LORD is the instruction of
wisdom; and before honour is humility.
PROVERBS 15:33

A man's pride shall bring him low:
but honour shall uphold the humble in spirit.
PROVERBS 29:23

Humble yourselves therefore under the mighty
hand of God, that he may exalt you in due time.
1 PETER 5:6

Lord, forever at Thy side
Let my place and portion be;
Strip me of the robe of pride,
Clothe me with humility.

"LORD, FOREVER AT THY SIDE," JAMES MONTGOMERY

JOY

Dear Lord, remind me to seek after true joy, knowing that happiness is often fleeting and never fulfilling. Let me draw a deep, deep joy from Your presence and find peace in that quiet place. Amen.

For ye shall go out with joy, and be led forth with peace: the mountains and the hills shall break forth before you into singing, and all the trees of the field shall clap their hands.
ISAIAH 55:12

Blessed is the people that know the joyful sound: they shall walk, O LORD, in the light of thy countenance. In thy name shall they rejoice all the day: and in thy righteousness shall they be exalted.
PSALM 89:15–16

The voice of rejoicing and salvation is in the tabernacles of the righteous: the right hand of the LORD doeth valiantly.
PSALM 118:15

Thou hast put gladness in my heart, more than in
the time that their corn and their wine increased.

PSALM 4:7

They that sow in tears shall reap in joy. He that goeth
forth and weepeth, bearing precious seed, shall doubtless
come again with rejoicing, bringing his sheaves with him.

PSALM 126:5–6

These things have I spoken unto you, that my joy
might remain in you, and that your joy might be full.

JOHN 15:11

Thou wilt shew me the path of life: in thy presence is fulness
of joy; at thy right hand there are pleasures for evermore.

PSALM 16:11

Light is sown for the righteous, and gladness for the
upright in heart. Rejoice in the LORD, ye righteous;
and give thanks at the remembrance of his holiness.

PSALM 97:11–12

Yet I will rejoice in the LORD,
I will joy in the God of my salvation.

HABAKKUK 3:18

106

Oh, weary pilgrim, lift your head:
For joy cometh in the morning!
For God in His own Word hath said
That joy cometh in the morning!

"JOY COMETH IN THE MORNING!" M. M. WIENLAND

Therefore the redeemed of the LORD shall return,
and come with singing unto Zion; and everlasting joy
shall be upon their head: they shall obtain gladness and joy;
and sorrow and mourning shall flee away.
ISAIAH 51:11

For our heart shall rejoice in him,
because we have trusted in his holy name.
PSALM 33:21

Whom having not seen, ye love; in whom,
though now ye see him not, yet believing,
ye rejoice with joy unspeakable and full of glory.
1 PETER 1:8

I will greatly rejoice in the LORD, my soul shall be joyful in my
God; for he hath clothed me with the garments of salvation,
he hath covered me with the robe of righteousness,
as a bridegroom decketh himself with ornaments,
and as a bride adorneth herself with her jewels.
ISAIAH 61:10

Then he said unto them, Go your way, eat the fat, and drink
the sweet, and send portions unto them for whom nothing is
prepared: for this day is holy unto our Lord: neither be
ye sorry; for the joy of the Lord is your strength.
NEHEMIAH 8:10

And thou shalt rejoice in the Lord,
and shalt glory in the Holy One of Israel.
ISAIAH 41:16

The righteous shall be glad in the Lord, and shall
trust in him; and all the upright in heart shall glory.
PSALM 64:10

My soul shall be satisfied as with marrow and fatness;
and my mouth shall praise thee with joyful lips.
PSALM 63:5

But let the righteous be glad; let them rejoice
before God: yea, let them exceedingly rejoice.
PSALM 68:3

I will see you again, and your heart shall rejoice,
and your joy no man taketh from you.
JOHN 16:22

O how happy are they
Who the Savior obey,
And have laid up their treasure above!
Tongue cannot express
The sweet comfort and peace
Of a soul in its earliest love.

"HOW HAPPY ARE THEY," CHARLES WESLEY

LAZINESS

-◆—•—◆-

Dear Lord, I struggle with discerning the difference between laziness and rest. Give me clarity when I don't know if I'm being lazy or if I just really need to sit down and take a break from work and the stresses in life. Amen.

And that ye study to be quiet, and to do your own business, and to work with your own hands, as we commanded you; that ye may walk honestly toward them that are without, and that ye may have lack of nothing.
1 Thessalonians 4:11–12

Not slothful in business;
fervent in spirit; serving the Lord.
Romans 12:11

He that tilleth his land shall have plenty of bread: but he that followeth after vain persons shall have poverty enough.
Proverbs 28:19

The soul of the sluggard desireth, and hath nothing:
but the soul of the diligent shall be made fat.
Proverbs 13:4

He becometh poor that dealeth with a slack hand:
but the hand of the diligent maketh rich.
He that gathereth in summer is a wise son:
but he that sleepeth in harvest is a son that causeth shame.
PROVERBS 10:4–5

Much food is in the tillage of the poor:
but there is that is destroyed for want of judgment.
PROVERBS 13:23

The husbandman that laboureth must be
first partaker of the fruits.
2 TIMOTHY 2:6

For even when we were with you, this we commanded you,
that if any would not work, neither should he eat. For we
hear that there are some which walk among you disorderly,
working not at all, but are busybodies. Now them that are such
we command and exhort by our Lord Jesus Christ, that with
quietness they work, and eat their own bread.
2 THESSALONIANS 3:10–12

Work ye, then, while yet 'tis day,
Work ye, Christians, while ye may,
Work for all that's great and good,
Working for your daily food.
Working whilst the golden hours,
Health, and strength, and youth are yours.

"WORK IS SWEET, FOR GOD HAS BLEST," GODFREY THRING

Love not sleep, lest thou come to poverty;
open thine eyes, and thou shalt be satisfied with bread.
PROVERBS 20:13

The way of the slothful man is as an hedge of thorns:
but the way of the righteous is made plain.
PROVERBS 15:19

Be thou diligent to know the state of thy flocks,
and look well to thy herds.
PROVERBS 27:23

The thoughts of the diligent tend only to plenteousness;
but of every one that is hasty only to want.
PROVERBS 21:5

The hand of the diligent shall bear rule:
but the slothful shall be under tribute.
PROVERBS 12:24

Let him that stole steal no more: but rather let him
labour, working with his hands the thing which is good,
that he may have to give to him that needeth.
EPHESIANS 4:28

He that tilleth his land shall be satisfied with bread:
but he that followeth vain persons is void of understanding.
PROVERBS 12:11

And thou shalt have goats' milk enough for thy
food, for the food of thy household, and for
the maintenance for thy maidens.

PROVERBS 27:27

O that I now the rest might know,
Believe, and enter in!
Now, Savior, now the power bestow,
And let me cease from sin.

"LORD, I BELIEVE A REST REMAINS," CHARLES WESLEY

LONELINESS

God, I often struggle with feelings of loneliness and the thought that I am the only one going through a particular situation. Whenever I become overwhelmed with these false thoughts, remind me that I am never alone, because You are always with me. Amen.

I will not leave you comfortless: I will come to you.
JOHN 14:18

Then shalt thou call, and the LORD shall answer;
thou shalt cry, and he shall say, Here I am.
ISAIAH 58:9

Since thou wast precious in my sight,
thou hast been honourable, and I have loved thee.
ISAIAH 43:4

And, behold, I am with thee, and will keep thee in
all places whither thou goest, and will bring thee
again into this land; for I will not leave thee, until I
have done that which I have spoken to thee of.
GENESIS 28:15

On life's pathway I am never lonely,
My Lord is with me, my Lord divine;
Ever-present guide, I trust Him only,
No longer lonely, for He is mine.

No longer lonely, no longer lonely,
For Jesus is the friend of friends to me;
No longer lonely, no longer lonely,
For Jesus is the friend of friends to me.

"No Longer Lonely," Robert Harkness

And will be a Father unto you, and ye shall be my
sons and daughters, saith the Lord Almighty.
2 Corinthians 6:18

And ye are complete in him, which is the
head of all principality and power.
Colossians 2:10

But I am poor and needy; yet the Lord thinketh
upon me: thou art my help and my deliverer;
make no tarrying, O my God.
Psalm 40:17

Hallelujah, 'tis done! I believe on the Son;
I am saved by the blood of the Crucified One;
Hallelujah, 'tis done! I believe on the Son;
I am saved by the blood of the Crucified One.

Though the pathway be lonely, and dangerous, too,
Surely Jesus is able to carry me through.

"HALLELUJAH, 'TIS DONE!" PHILIP P. BLISS

....
....
....
....
....
....
....
....
....
....
....
....
....
....
....
....

LONG LIFE

Lord, there is no promise of a long life, but there is the much better promise of eternal life because of Your sacrifice for our sins. I want to live each day with that in mind and to treasure the time on earth that You have given me—before I come home to live in my "forever home" with You. Amen.

And even to your old age I am he; and even
to hoar hairs will I carry you: I have made,
and I will bear; even I will carry, and will deliver you.
ISAIAH 46:4

With the ancient is wisdom; and in length of
days understanding. With him is wisdom and
strength, he hath counsel and understanding.
JOB 12:12–13

The glory of young men is their strength:
and the beauty of old men is the grey head.
PROVERBS 20:29

Children's children are the crown of old men;
and the glory of children are their fathers.
PROVERBS 17:6

The hoary head is a crown of glory,
if it be found in the way of righteousness.
PROVERBS 16:31

And thine age shall be clearer than the noonday:
thou shalt shine forth, thou shalt be as the morning.
JOB 11:17

My son, forget not my law; but let thine heart
keep my commandments: for length of days,
and long life, and peace, shall they add to thee.
PROVERBS 3:1–2

Cast me not off in the time of old age;
forsake me not when my strength faileth.
PSALM 71:9

Take my life and let it be consecrated, Lord, to Thee.
Take my moments and my days; let them flow in ceaseless praise.
Take my hands and let them move at the impulse of Thy love.
Take my feet and let them be swift and beautiful for Thee.

"TAKE MY LIFE AND LET IT BE," FRANCES R. HAVERGAL

O God, thou hast taught me from my youth: and hitherto
have I declared thy wondrous works. Now also when I am
old and greyheaded, O God, forsake me not; until I have
shewed thy strength unto this generation, and thy
power to every one that is to come.
PSALM 71:17–18

LORD, make me to know mine end, and the measure of
my days, what it is: that I may know how frail I am.
Behold, thou hast made my days as an handbreadth;
and mine age is as nothing before thee.
PSALM 39:4–5

Ye shall walk in all the ways which the LORD your God
hath commanded you, that ye may live, and that it may
be well with you, and that ye may prolong your days
in the land which ye shall possess.
DEUTERONOMY 5:33

With long life will I satisfy him,
and shew him my salvation.
PSALM 91:16

That thou mightest fear the LORD thy God, to keep all
his statutes and his commandments, which I command thee,
thou, and thy son, and thy son's son, all the days of thy life;
and that thy days may be prolonged.
DEUTERONOMY 6:2

The fear of the LORD prolongeth days:
but the years of the wicked shall be shortened.
PROVERBS 10:27

For by me thy days shall be multiplied,
and the years of thy life shall be increased.
PROVERBS 9:11

If you ask me why I'm happy as I journey down life's road,
Why it is I do not carry on the way a heavy load,
'Tis because my Savior tells me that my burden He'll receive.
And I believe it, every word I believe.

"EVERY WORD I BELIEVE," JOHNSON OATMAN JR.

LOVE, BROTHERLY

-+- • -+-

Lord, it isn't always easy to love others—in fact,
this loving others is a pretty tough business!
Whenever I am frustrated with a family member
or friend, I need to remember that they are my
brothers and sisters in Christ. Please help me
reflect Your love to everyone I meet. Amen.

A new commandment I give unto you, That ye love one
another; as I have loved you, that ye also love one another.
By this shall all men know that ye are my disciples,
if ye have love one to another.
JOHN 13:34–35

Let love be without dissimulation. Abhor that which is evil;
cleave to that which is good. Be kindly affectioned one to
another with brotherly love; in honour preferring one another.
ROMANS 12:9–10

But as touching brotherly love ye need not
that I write unto you: for ye yourselves are
taught of God to love one another.
1 THESSALONIANS 4:9

He that loveth his brother abideth in the light,
and there is none occasion of stumbling in him.
1 JOHN 2:10

Seeing ye have purified your souls in obeying the truth through
the Spirit unto unfeigned love of the brethren, see that ye love
one another with a pure heart fervently.
1 PETER 1:22

Truthful Spirit, dwell with me!
I myself would truthful be;
And with wisdom kind and clear
Let Thy life in mine appear;
And with actions brotherly
Speak my Lord's sincerity.

"GRACIOUS SPIRIT, DWELL WITH ME," THOMAS T. LYNCH

My little children, let us not love in word,
neither in tongue; but in deed and in truth.
1 JOHN 3:18

Beloved, if God so loved us,
we ought also to love one another.
1 JOHN 4:11

Beloved, let us love one another: for love is of God;
and every one that loveth is born of God, and knoweth God.
He that loveth not knoweth not God; for God is love.
1 JOHN 4:7–8

Put on therefore, as the elect of God, holy and beloved, bowels of mercies, kindness, humbleness of mind, meekness, longsuffering; forbearing one another, and forgiving one another, if any man have a quarrel against any: even as Christ forgave you, so also do ye.

COLOSSIANS 3:12–13

To labor and to love,
To pardon and endure,
To lift thy heart to God above,
And keep thy conscience pure.

"BELIEVE NOT THOSE WHO SAY," ANNE BRONTË

....
....
....
....
....
....
....
....
....
....
....
....

123

LOVE, GOD'S

—◆———•———◆—

Heavenly Father, Your love knows no bounds. I can't even fathom how deeply and truly You love me. Thank You for Your eternal, unconditional love and for the ways You show me that love every day and in so many ways. Amen.

For God so loved the world, that he gave his only begotten Son, that whosoever believeth in him should not perish, but have everlasting life.
JOHN 3:16

And he will love thee, and bless thee, and multiply thee: he will also bless the fruit of thy womb, and the fruit of thy land, thy corn, and thy wine, and thine oil, the increase of thy kine, and the flocks of thy sheep, in the land which he sware unto thy fathers to give thee.
DEUTERONOMY 7:13

The LORD openeth the eyes of the blind: the LORD raiseth them that are bowed down: the LORD loveth the righteous.
PSALM 146:8

The way of the wicked is an abomination unto the LORD:
but he loveth him that followeth after righteousness.
PROVERBS 15:9

For as a young man marrieth a virgin, so shall thy sons
marry thee: and as the bridegroom rejoiceth over
the bride, so shall thy God rejoice over thee.
ISAIAH 62:5

Herein is love, not that we loved God, but that he loved us,
and sent his Son to be the propitiation for our sins.
1 JOHN 4:10

I will heal their backsliding, I will love them freely:
for mine anger is turned away from him.
HOSEA 14:4

The LORD thy God in the midst of thee is mighty;
he will save, he will rejoice over thee with joy;
he will rest in his love, he will joy over thee with singing.
ZEPHANIAH 3:17

The LORD hath appeared of old unto me, saying,
Yea, I have loved thee with an everlasting love:
therefore with lovingkindness have I drawn thee.
JEREMIAH 31:3

The love of God is greater far
Than tongue or pen can ever tell;
It goes beyond the highest star,
And reaches to the lowest hell;
The guilty pair, bowed down with care,
God gave His Son to win;
His erring child He reconciled,
And pardoned from his sin.

"THE LOVE OF GOD," FREDERICK M. LEHMAN

And I have declared unto them thy name,
and will declare it: that the love wherewith thou
hast loved me may be in them, and I in them.
JOHN 17:26

Yea, I will rejoice over them to do them good,
and I will plant them in this land assuredly
with my whole heart and with my whole soul.
JEREMIAH 32:41

And we have known and believed the love that God
hath to us. God is love; and he that dwelleth in
love dwelleth in God, and God in him.
1 JOHN 4:16

We love him, because he first loved us.
1 JOHN 4:19

For the Father himself loveth you, because ye have loved me, and have believed that I came out from God.
JOHN 16:27

I in them, and thou in me, that they may be made perfect in one; and that the world may know that thou hast sent me, and hast loved them, as thou hast loved me.
JOHN 17:23

Now our Lord Jesus Christ himself, and God, even our Father, which hath loved us, and hath given us everlasting consolation and good hope through grace, comfort your hearts, and stablish you in every good word and work.
2 THESSALONIANS 2:16–17

Come quickly in, Thou heavenly guest,
Nor ever hence remove;
But sup with us, and let the feast
Be everlasting love.

"COME, LET US WHO IN CHRIST BELIEVE," CHARLES WESLEY

....
....
....
....
....
....
....

LOVING GOD

Lord, You have promised that those who seek You shall find You. Thank You for never breaking that promise and for showing that You are a loving God. You are the perfect example of love, and I hope to always show that to others. Amen.

Know therefore that the LORD thy God, he is God, the faithful God, which keepeth covenant and mercy with them that love him and keep his commandments to a thousand generations.
DEUTERONOMY 7:9

I love them that love me;
and those that seek me early shall find me.
PROVERBS 8:17

He that hath my commandments, and keepeth them,
he it is that loveth me: and he that loveth me shall
be loved of my Father, and I will love him,
and will manifest myself to him.
JOHN 14:21

That I may cause those that love me to inherit
substance; and I will fill their treasures.
PROVERBS 8:21

Delight thyself also in the LORD:
and he shall give thee the desires of thine heart.
PSALM 37:4

Come quickly, then, my Lord, and take
Possession of Thine own;
My longing heart vouchsafe to make
Thine everlasting throne.

Assert Thy claim, receive Thy right,
Come quickly from above,
And sink me to perfection's height,
The depth of humble love.

"WHAT SHALL I DO, MY GOD TO LOVE?" CHARLES WESLEY

Because he hath set his love upon me,
therefore will I deliver him: I will set him on high,
because he hath known my name.
PSALM 91:14

But as it is written, Eye hath not seen, nor ear heard,
neither have entered into the heart of man, the things
which God hath prepared for them that love him.
1 CORINTHIANS 2:9

The LORD preserveth all them that love him:
but all the wicked will he destroy.
PSALM 145:20

Grace be with all them that love
our Lord Jesus Christ in sincerity. Amen.
EPHESIANS 6:24

Oh, Jesus' light and boundless grace!
How blest was I to see His face,
His life He did not spare;
This sinner He in love did seek,
Enabling me His Word to speak,
I walk as child and heir.

"THE GOD OF HOLINESS AND LOVE," DANIEL BORGES

LUST

Lord, You gave us desires and also explained how those desires could be glorifying to You. Help me to keep my thoughts and desires under control. . .rather than letting them control me. Help me submit them all to You. Amen.

For all that is in the world, the lust of the flesh,
and the lust of the eyes, and the pride of life,
is not of the Father, but is of the world.
And the world passeth away, and the lust thereof:
but he that doeth the will of God abideth for ever.
1 John 2:16–17

Ye have heard that it was said by them of old time,
Thou shalt not commit adultery: but I say unto you,
That whosoever looketh on a woman to lust after her
hath committed adultery with her already in his heart.
Matthew 5:27–28

Whereby are given unto us exceeding great and
precious promises: that by these ye might be partakers
of the divine nature, having escaped the corruption
that is in the world through lust.
2 Peter 1:4

Lust not after her beauty in thine heart; neither let her take thee with her eyelids. For by means of a whorish woman a man is brought to a piece of bread: and the adultress will hunt for the precious life. Can a man take fire in his bosom, and his clothes not be burned? Can one go upon hot coals, and his feet not be burned? So he that goeth in to his neighbour's wife; whosoever toucheth her shall not be innocent.

PROVERBS 6:25–29

Submit yourselves therefore to God. Resist the devil, and he will flee from you. Draw nigh to God, and he will draw nigh to you. Cleanse your hands, ye sinners; and purify your hearts, ye double minded.

JAMES 4:7–8

Dearly beloved, I beseech you as strangers and pilgrims, abstain from fleshly lusts, which war against the soul.

1 PETER 2:11

As obedient children, not fashioning yourselves according to the former lusts in your ignorance: but as he which hath called you is holy, so be ye holy in all manner of conversation; because it is written, Be ye holy; for I am holy.

1 PETER 1:14–16

And they that are Christ's have crucified the flesh with the affections and lusts.

GALATIANS 5:24

For we ourselves also were sometimes foolish, disobedient, deceived, serving divers lusts and pleasures, living in malice and envy, hateful, and hating one another. But after that the kindness and love of God our Saviour toward man appeared, not by works of righteousness which we have done, but according to his mercy he saved us, by the washing of regeneration, and renewing of the Holy Ghost.
TITUS 3:3–5

For the grace of God that bringeth salvation hath appeared to all men, teaching us that, denying ungodliness and worldly lusts, we should live soberly, righteously, and godly, in this present world.
TITUS 2:11–12

Flee also youthful lusts: but follow righteousness, faith, charity, peace, with them that call on the Lord out of a pure heart.
2 TIMOTHY 2:22

Likewise reckon ye also yourselves to be dead indeed unto
sin, but alive unto God through Jesus Christ our Lord.
Let not sin therefore reign in your mortal body,
that ye should obey it in the lusts thereof. . . .
For sin shall not have dominion over you:
for ye are not under the law, but under grace.
ROMANS 6:11–12, 14

My sins have taken such a hold on me,
I am not able to look up to Thee;
Lord, I repent; accept my tears and grief:
But Thou hast taken all my sins away,
And I in Thee dare now look up and pray:
Lord, I believe; help Thou mine unbelief.

"MY SINS HAVE TAKEN SUCH A HOLD ON ME," JOHN S. B. MONSELL

LYING

Dear God, honesty is a character trait that You value so highly; yet lying comes so naturally to me. I want to be honest and to speak the truth, even when it's difficult. Give me the strength and integrity to speak the truth in every situation. Amen.

Lie not one to another, seeing that ye have put off the old man with his deeds; and have put on the new man, which is renewed in knowledge after the image of him that created him.
COLOSSIANS 3:9–10

And ye shall not swear by my name falsely, neither shalt thou profane the name of thy God: I am the LORD.
LEVITICUS 19:12

A man that beareth false witness against his neighbour is a maul, and a sword, and a sharp arrow.
PROVERBS 25:18

A faithful witness will not lie:
but a false witness will utter lies.
PROVERBS 14:5

135

Thou shalt not raise a false report: put not thine
hand with the wicked to be an unrighteous witness.
EXODUS 23:1

A false witness shall not be unpunished,
and he that speaketh lies shall not escape.
PROVERBS 19:5

———————

Ring out false pride in place and blood,
The civic slander and the spite;
Ring in the love of truth and right,
Ring in the common love of good.

"RING OUT THE OLD, RING IN THE NEW," ALFRED TENNYSON

———————

But the fearful, and unbelieving, and the abominable,
and murderers, and whoremongers, and sorcerers,
and idolaters, and all liars, shall have their part in the lake
which burneth with fire and brimstone:
which is the second death.
REVELATION 21:8

A false witness shall not be unpunished,
and he that speaketh lies shall perish.
PROVERBS 19:9

Be not a witness against thy neighbour
without cause; and deceive not with thy lips.
PROVERBS 24:28

The wicked are estranged from the womb:
they go astray as soon as they be born, speaking lies.
PSALM 58:3

But if ye have bitter envying and strife in your hearts,
glory not, and lie not against the truth.
JAMES 3:14

The lip of truth shall be established for ever:
but a lying tongue is but for a moment.
PROVERBS 12:19

Then let us sit beneath His cross,
And gladly catch the healing stream:
All things for Him account but loss,
And give up all our hearts to Him:
Of nothing think or speak beside,
My Lord, my love, is crucified!

"O LOVE DIVINE, WHAT HAST THOU DONE," CHARLES WESLEY

....
....
....
....
....
....
....

MARRIAGE

Lord, You created marriage and blessed it. When, at times, loving my spouse doesn't come naturally and I have to choose to love him, give me the patience and determination I need to work at the relationship. Help me to be humble, putting him before myself. Amen.

Live joyfully with the wife whom thou lovest all the days of the life of thy vanity, which he hath given thee under the sun, all the days of thy vanity: for that is thy portion in this life, and in thy labour which thou takest under the sun.
ECCLESIASTES 9:9

Drink waters out of thine own cistern,
and running waters out of thine own well.
PROVERBS 5:15

Let thy fountain be blessed: and rejoice with the wife of thy youth. Let her be as the loving hind and pleasant roe; let her breasts satisfy thee at all times; and be thou ravished always with her love. And why wilt thou, my son, be ravished with a strange woman, and embrace the bosom of a stranger?
PROVERBS 5:18–20

Let the husband render unto the wife due benevolence:
and likewise also the wife unto the husband.
1 CORINTHIANS 7:3

Wives, submit yourselves unto your own husbands, as unto the
Lord. For the husband is the head of the wife, even as Christ
is the head of the church: and he is the saviour of the body.
EPHESIANS 5:22–23

Husbands, love your wives, even as Christ
also loved the church, and gave himself for it.
EPHESIANS 5:25

So ought men to love their wives as their own bodies.
He that loveth his wife loveth himself.
EPHESIANS 5:28

———————————

*Savior, let Thy sanction rest
On the union witnessed now;
Be it with Thy presence blest;
Ratify the nuptial vow;
Hallowed let this union be
With each other, and with Thee.*

"SAVIOR, LET THY SANCTION REST," THOMAS RAFFLES

———————————

139

For this cause shall a man leave his father and mother,
and shall be joined unto his wife, and they two shall be one flesh.
EPHESIANS 5:31

Nevertheless let every one of you in particular
so love his wife even as himself; and the wife
see that she reverence her husband.
EPHESIANS 5:33

But if any provide not for his own, and specially
for those of his own house, he hath denied
the faith, and is worse than an infidel.
1 TIMOTHY 5:8

Wives, submit yourselves unto your own husbands,
as it is fit in the Lord. Husbands, love your wives,
and be not bitter against them.
COLOSSIANS 3:18–19

Likewise, ye husbands, dwell with them according to
knowledge, giving honour unto the wife, as unto the
weaker vessel, and as being heirs together of the
grace of life; that your prayers be not hindered.
1 PETER 3:7

That they may teach the young women to be sober,
to love their husbands, to love their children,
to be discreet, chaste, keepers at home, good, obedient to their
own husbands, that the word of God be not blasphemed.
TITUS 2:4–5

I'm invited to a supper,
'Tis a marriage feast and grand,
'Tis the greatest of all banquets
Ever known on sea or land;
There will be a countless host of guests,
The Bridegroom and the Bride,
And all who to this supper go,
On shining clouds shall ride.

"THE MARRIAGE SUPPER," FREDERICK E. RIMANOCZY

MEEKNESS

❖━━━━━━•━━━━━━❖

Heavenly Father, meekness is not an attribute that is highly regarded; it isn't valued very much, and it's hard to live out in daily life. You have given me such a good example of meekness, Lord. Please help me to have a mild disposition. Thank You, Lord. Amen.

Blessed are the meek: for they shall inherit the earth.
MATTHEW 5:5

But with righteousness shall he judge the poor,
and reprove with equity for the meek of the earth.
ISAIAH 11:4

The meek also shall increase their joy in the LORD,
and the poor among men shall rejoice in the
Holy One of Israel.
ISAIAH 29:19

The LORD lifteth up the meek:
he casteth the wicked down to the ground.
PSALM 147:6

The meek will he guide in judgment:
and the meek will he teach his way.
PSALM 25:9

But the meek shall inherit the earth; and shall
delight themselves in the abundance of peace.
PSALM 37:11

Loving Jesus, gentle Lamb,
In Thy gracious hands I am;
Make me, Savior, what Thou art,
Live Thyself within my heart.

"GENTLE JESUS, MEEK AND MILD," CHARLES WESLEY

A soft answer turneth away wrath:
but grievous words stir up anger.
PROVERBS 15:1

Seek ye the LORD, all ye meek of the earth, which have
wrought his judgment; seek righteousness, seek meekness:
it may be ye shall be hid in the day of the LORD's anger.
ZEPHANIAH 2:3

But let it be the hidden man of the heart, in that which is not
corruptible, even the ornament of a meek and quiet spirit,
which is in the sight of God of great price.
1 PETER 3:4

The meek shall eat and be satisfied:
they shall praise the LORD that seek him:
your heart shall live for ever.
PSALM 22:26

For the LORD taketh pleasure in his people:
he will beautify the meek with salvation.
PSALM 149:4

Meekly may my soul receive
All Thy Spirit hath revealed;
Thou hast spoken; I believe,
Though the prophecy were sealed.

"LORD, FOREVER AT THY SIDE," JAMES MONTGOMERY

MERCY

Lord, mercy is a foreign concept in today's world. We want everything to be fair, but if that were really the case, there would be no hope. I am thankful each day for the grace You have given me. Help me to be merciful to those who are undeserving and to give them the same grace You have extended to me. Amen.

And therefore will the LORD wait, that he may be gracious unto you, and therefore will he be exalted, that he may have mercy upon you: for the LORD is a God of judgment: blessed are all they that wait for him.
ISAIAH 30:18

And the LORD passed by before him, and proclaimed, The LORD, The LORD God, merciful and gracious, longsuffering, and abundant in goodness and truth, keeping mercy for thousands, forgiving iniquity and transgression and sin, and that will by no means clear the guilty; visiting the iniquity of the fathers upon the children, and upon the children's children, unto the third and to the fourth generation.
EXODUS 34:6–7

Like as a father pitieth his children,
so the LORD pitieth them that fear him.
PSALM 103:13

But the mercy of the LORD is from everlasting
to everlasting upon them that fear him,
and his righteousness unto children's children.
PSALM 103:17

There's a wideness in God's mercy,
Like the wideness of the sea;
There's a kindness in His justice,
Which is more than liberty.

"THERE'S A WIDENESS IN GOD'S MERCY," FREDERICK W. FABER

And he said, I will make all my goodness pass before thee,
and I will proclaim the name of the LORD before thee;
and will be gracious to whom I will be gracious,
and will shew mercy on whom I will shew mercy.
EXODUS 33:19

And I will have mercy upon her that had not obtained mercy;
and I will say to them which were not my people, Thou art
my people; and they shall say, Thou art my God.
HOSEA 2:23

For in my wrath I smote thee,
but in my favour have I had mercy on thee.
ISAIAH 60:10

For my name's sake will I defer mine anger, and for my
praise will I refrain for thee, that I cut thee not off.
ISAIAH 48:9

O sing the greatness of His mercy,
Unto those that seek Him ever full and free;
O sing, while angels join the chorus,
Rolling onward like the sea.

"THE GREATNESS OF HIS MERCY," FANNY CROSBY

MONEY

—◆———•———◆—

Dear God, sometimes it seems like money really could buy happiness. . .that everything in my life would be easier if I had just a little bit more of it. Whenever I have these thoughts, remind me that the love of money is the root of all evil and that true happiness only comes from You. Amen.

Labour not to be rich: cease from thine own wisdom.
Wilt thou set thine eyes upon that which is not?
for riches certainly make themselves wings;
they fly away as an eagle toward heaven.
PROVERBS 23:4–5

A little that a righteous man hath is better
than the riches of many wicked.
PSALM 37:16

Hearken, my beloved brethren, Hath not God chosen the
poor of this world rich in faith, and heirs of the kingdom
which he hath promised to them that love him?
JAMES 2:5

Better is an handful with quietness,
than both the hands full with travail and vexation of spirit.
ECCLESIASTES 4:6

For the oppression of the poor, for the sighing of
the needy, now will I arise, saith the LORD;
I will set him in safety from him that puffeth at him.
PSALM 12:5

Whoso mocketh the poor reproacheth his Maker:
and he that is glad at calamities shall not be unpunished.
PROVERBS 17:5

Both riches and honour come of thee, and thou reignest
over all; and in thine hand is power and might; and in thine
hand it is to make great, and to give strength unto all.
1 CHRONICLES 29:12

Rob not the poor, because he is poor:
neither oppress the afflicted in the gate.
PROVERBS 22:22

Charge them that are rich in this world, that they be
not highminded, nor trust in uncertain riches,
but in the living God, who giveth us richly all things to enjoy;
that they do good, that they be rich in good works,
ready to distribute, willing to communicate;
laying up in store for themselves a good foundation against
the time to come, that they may lay hold on eternal life.
1 TIMOTHY 6:17–19

He that trusteth in his riches shall fall;
but the righteous shall flourish as a branch.
PROVERBS 11:28

The sleep of a labouring man is sweet, whether he eat little
or much: but the abundance of the rich will not suffer him
to sleep. There is a sore evil which I have seen under the sun,
namely, riches kept for the owners thereof to their hurt.
But those riches perish by evil travail: and he begetteth a son,
and there is nothing in his hand.

ECCLESIASTES 5:12–14

But thou shalt remember the LORD thy God:
for it is he that giveth thee power to get wealth,
that he may establish his covenant which he sware
unto thy fathers, as it is this day.

DEUTERONOMY 8:18

Better is little with the fear of the LORD
than great treasure and trouble therewith.

PROVERBS 15:16

The rich and poor meet together:
the LORD is the maker of them all.

PROVERBS 22:2

Lift up your hearts to things above,
Ye followers of the Lamb,
And join with us to praise His love,
And glorify His name.

"LIFT UP YOUR HEARTS TO THINGS ABOVE," CHARLES WESLEY

For the needy shall not always be forgotten:
the expectation of the poor shall not perish for ever.
PSALM 9:18

A faithful man shall abound with blessings:
but he that maketh haste to be rich shall not be innocent.
PROVERBS 28:20

Riches profit not in the day of wrath:
but righteousness delivereth from death.
PROVERBS 11:4

They shall cast their silver in the streets, and their gold
shall be removed: their silver and their gold shall not be able
to deliver them in the day of the wrath of the LORD: they shall
not satisfy their souls, neither fill their bowels:
because it is the stumblingblock of their iniquity.
EZEKIEL 7:19

There is that maketh himself rich, yet hath nothing:
there is that maketh himself poor, yet hath great riches.
PROVERBS 13:7

He that loveth silver shall not be satisfied with silver;
nor he that loveth abundance with increase: this is also vanity.
ECCLESIASTES 5:10

For we brought nothing into this world,
and it is certain we can carry nothing out.
1 TIMOTHY 6:7

He that oppresseth the poor to increase his riches,
and he that giveth to the rich, shall surely come to want.
PROVERBS 22:16

He that hasteth to be rich hath an evil eye,
and considereth not that poverty shall come upon him.
PROVERBS 28:22

Better is the poor that walketh in his uprightness,
than he that is perverse in his ways, though he be rich.
PROVERBS 28:6

Blessed is he that considereth the poor:
the LORD will deliver him in time of trouble.
PSALM 41:1

The grandeur of wealth, and the temples of fame,
Where beauty and splendor combine,
Will perish, forgotten, and crumble to dust,
But they that be wise shall shine.

"THEY THAT BE WISE," FANNY CROSBY

OBEDIENCE

*Abba Father, obedience doesn't come naturally to me.
I can be so stubborn and determined to have my
way that I forget that Your will should trump mine.
Give me an obedient heart, Lord, one that wants
to serve You and glorify You in every way. Amen.*

See, I have set before thee this day life and good, and death
and evil; in that I command thee this day to love the LORD thy
God, to walk in his ways, and to keep his commandments and
his statutes and his judgments, that thou mayest live and
multiply: and the LORD thy God shall bless thee in the
land whither thou goest to possess it.
DEUTERONOMY 30:15–16

And thou shalt do that which is right and good in the
sight of the LORD: that it may be well with thee, and that
thou mayest go in and possess the good land which
the LORD sware unto thy fathers.
DEUTERONOMY 6:18

Keep therefore the words of this covenant,
and do them, that ye may prosper in all that ye do.
DEUTERONOMY 29:9

Hear therefore, O Israel, and observe to do it; that it may
be well with thee, and that ye may increase mightily,
as the LORD God of thy fathers hath promised thee,
in the land that floweth with milk and honey.
DEUTERONOMY 6:3

Wherefore it shall come to pass, if ye hearken to these
judgments, and keep, and do them, that the LORD thy
God shall keep unto thee the covenant and the
mercy which he sware unto thy fathers.
DEUTERONOMY 7:12

O that there were such an heart in them, that they would fear
me, and keep all my commandments always, that it might be
well with them, and with their children for ever!
DEUTERONOMY 5:29

Those things, which ye have both learned,
and received, and heard, and seen in me, do:
and the God of peace shall be with you.
PHILIPPIANS 4:9

Whosoever therefore shall break one of these
least commandments, and shall teach men so,
he shall be called the least in the kingdom of heaven:
but whosoever shall do and teach them, the same
shall be called great in the kingdom of heaven.
MATTHEW 5:19

Therefore whosoever heareth these sayings of mine,
and doeth them, I will liken him unto a wise man,
which built his house upon a rock: and the rain descended, and
the floods came, and the winds blew, and beat upon that house;
and it fell not: for it was founded upon a rock.
MATTHEW 7:24–25

Jesus answered and said unto him, If a man love me,
he will keep my words: and my Father will love him,
and we will come unto him, and make our abode with him.
JOHN 14:23

And we know that all things work together for
good to them that love God, to them who
are the called according to his purpose.
ROMANS 8:28

For not the hearers of the law are just before God,
but the doers of the law shall be justified.
ROMANS 2:13

Master, speak! Thy servant heareth,
Waiting for Thy gracious word,
Longing for Thy voice that cheereth;
Master! let it now be heard.
I am listening, Lord, for Thee:
What hast Thou to say to me?

"MASTER, SPEAK! THY SERVANT HEARETH," FRANCES R. HAVERGAL

If ye know these things,
happy are ye if ye do them.
JOHN 13:17

If ye keep my commandments, ye shall abide
in my love; even as I have kept my Father's
commandments, and abide in his love.
JOHN 15:10

But whoso looketh into the perfect law of liberty,
and continueth therein, he being not a forgetful hearer,
but a doer of the work, this man shall be blessed in his deed.
JAMES 1:25

Verily, verily, I say unto you, He that heareth my word,
and believeth on him that sent me, hath everlasting life,
and shall not come into condemnation;
but is passed from death unto life.
JOHN 5:24

For whosoever shall do the will of my Father
which is in heaven, the same is my brother,
and sister, and mother.
MATTHEW 12:50

And the world passeth away, and the lust thereof:
but he that doeth the will of God abideth for ever.
1 JOHN 2:17

Not every one that saith unto me, Lord,
Lord, shall enter into the kingdom of heaven;
but he that doeth the will of my Father which is in heaven.
MATTHEW 7:21

And whatsoever we ask, we receive of him,
because we keep his commandments,
and do those things that are pleasing in his sight.
1 JOHN 3:22

Our Father, Thou in Heav'n above,
Who biddest us to dwell in love,
As brethren of one family,
To cry in every need to Thee,
Teach us no thoughtless words to say,
But from our inmost heart to pray.

"OUR FATHER, THOU IN HEAVEN ABOVE," MARTIN LUTHER

PARENTS' DUTIES

—◆———•———◆—

Lord, being a parent is probably one of the most difficult jobs in the world. Selflessness and unconditional love are required, and those definitely don't come naturally. When good parenting becomes a challenge for me, remind me of Your perfect example. Amen.

For I know him, that he will command his children and his household after him, and they shall keep the way of the LORD, to do justice and judgment.
GENESIS 18:19

And thou shalt shew thy son in that day, saying, This is done because of that which the LORD did unto me when I came forth out of Egypt.
EXODUS 13:8

And, ye fathers, provoke not your children to wrath: but bring them up in the nurture and admonition of the Lord.
EPHESIANS 6:4

Fathers, provoke not your children to anger, lest they be discouraged.
COLOSSIANS 3:21

Children, in years and knowledge young,
Your parents' hope, your parents' joy,
Attend the counsels of my tongue,
Let pious thoughts your minds employ.

"CHILDREN, IN YEARS AND KNOWLEDGE YOUNG," ISAAC WATTS

Only take heed to thyself, and keep thy soul diligently,
lest thou forget the things which thine eyes have seen,
and lest they depart from thy heart all the days of thy life:
but teach them thy sons, and thy sons' sons. . .Gather me
the people together, and I will make them hear my words,
that they may learn to fear me all the days that they shall live
upon the earth, and that they may teach their children.
DEUTERONOMY 4:9–10

Train up a child in the way he should go:
and when he is old, he will not depart from it.
PROVERBS 22:6

And ye shall teach them your children, speaking of them
when thou sittest in thine house, and when thou walkest
by the way, when thou liest down, and when thou risest up.
DEUTERONOMY 11:19

Correct thy son, and he shall give thee rest; yea,
he shall give delight unto thy soul.
PROVERBS 29:17

O help us through the prayer of faith
More firmly to believe;
For still the more the servant hath,
The more shall he receive.

"O HELP US LORD, EACH HOUR OF NEED," HENRY H. MILMAN

PATIENCE

Dear God, I find myself wanting everything "right now," as quickly as possible. I know that You bless those who wait and honor You with their patience. Please help me to have patience—whether I'm waiting in line for my latte or asking You to provide a new job. Thank You, Father. Amen.

Be patient therefore, brethren, unto the coming of the Lord. Behold, the husbandman waiteth for the precious fruit of the earth, and hath long patience for it, until he receive the early and latter rain. Be ye also patient; stablish your hearts: for the coming of the Lord draweth nigh.
JAMES 5:7–8

For what glory is it, if, when ye be buffeted for your faults, ye shall take it patiently? but if, when ye do well, and suffer for it, ye take it patiently, this is acceptable with God.
1 PETER 2:20

And let us not be weary in well doing:
for in due season we shall reap, if we faint not.
GALATIANS 6:9

Let us hold fast the profession of our faith
without wavering; (for he is faithful that promised).
HEBREWS 10:23

But he that shall endure unto the end,
the same shall be saved.
MATTHEW 24:13

Life is oft beset with sorrows,
Trials come on every hand;
Fain would careworn pilgrims borrow
Pleasures from the glory land;
But we bide our time with patience,
Waiting till our Lord shall come,
Waiting till the Master bids us
Enter our eternal home.

"WILL HE BID US ENTER IN?" W. B. CARNES

That ye be not slothful, but followers of them who
through faith and patience inherit the promises.
HEBREWS 6:12

My brethren, count it all joy when ye fall into divers
temptations; knowing this, that the trying of your faith
worketh patience. But let patience have her perfect work,
that ye may be perfect and entire, wanting nothing.
JAMES 1:2–4

For ye have need of patience, that, after ye have
done the will of God, ye might receive the promise.
HEBREWS 10:36

And not only so, but we glory in tribulations also:
knowing that tribulation worketh patience;
and patience, experience; and experience, hope.
ROMANS 5:3–4

He lives, our great Redeemer lives!
And we who now believe,
And bear the cross with patience here,
Shall life through Him receive.
Our thankful hearts adore His love,
Our souls with rapture sing.

"WHERE IS THY STING?" FANNY CROSBY

PEACE

❦ • ❦

Heavenly Father, the peace You provide passes all
understanding and cannot be found anywhere
else. When I turn to temporary sources of peace
and am unsatisfied, lead me back to You.
Comfort me in my distress, Lord. Amen.

Peace, peace to him that is far off, and to him
that is near, saith the LORD; and I will heal him.
ISAIAH 57:19

And let the peace of God rule in your hearts, to the
which also ye are called in one body; and be ye thankful.
COLOSSIANS 3:15

I will hear what God the LORD will speak: for he
will speak peace unto his people, and to his saints.
PSALM 85:8

And the peace of God, which passeth all understanding,
shall keep your hearts and minds through Christ Jesus.
PHILIPPIANS 4:7

Peace, peace, wonderful peace,
Coming down from the Father above!
Sweep over my spirit forever, I pray,
In fathomless billows of love!

"WONDERFUL PEACE," WARREN D. CORNELL

And the work of righteousness shall be peace;
and the effect of righteousness quietness and assurance for ever.
ISAIAH 32:17

Thy faith hath saved thee; go in peace.
LUKE 7:50

Mark the perfect man, and behold the upright:
for the end of that man is peace.
PSALM 37:37

Now the Lord of peace himself give you peace
always by all means.
2 THESSALONIANS 3:16

Peace I leave with you, my peace I give unto you:
not as the world giveth, give I unto you.
Let not your heart be troubled, neither let it be afraid.
JOHN 14:27

I believe the Bible, it taught me how to pray,
Jesus heard and answered, took my sins away;
Gave me peace and pardon, wrote my name above,
Glory hallelujah! for His wondrous love.

"I Believe the Bible," Edwin S. Ufford and Wenford G. Schurman

POVERTY

*Lord, You promise to give me what I need;
however, You do not promise to give me what I want.
When times are tough and I have to give up
things that aren't necessary, help me to remember
Your promise and to not give up hope. Amen.*

For he shall deliver the needy when he crieth;
the poor also, and him that hath no helper.
He shall spare the poor and needy,
and shall save the souls of the needy.
PSALM 72:12–13

Yet setteth he the poor on high from affliction,
and maketh him families like a flock.
PSALM 107:41

For the LORD heareth the poor,
and despiseth not his prisoners.
PSALM 69:33

Sing unto the LORD, praise ye the LORD:
for he hath delivered the soul of the
poor from the hand of evildoers.
JEREMIAH 20:13

He will regard the prayer of the destitute,
and not despise their prayer.
PSALM 102:17

He raiseth up the poor out of the dust,
and lifteth the needy out of the dunghill.
PSALM 113:7

I will abundantly bless her provision:
I will satisfy her poor with bread.
PSALM 132:15

Thou, O God, hast prepared of
thy goodness for the poor.
PSALM 68:10

Let all praise the Lord for His goodness and mercy,
He's more to me now than the loved ones of yore;
Surprising me daily with fresh gifts from Heaven,
His kingly provision is mine more and more.

"THE CONQUEROR'S TREAD," FLORENCE POTTER

PRAYER

—◆———•———◆—

Lord, I want to think of prayer as a constant conversation between me and You. But most of the time I find myself halfheartedly squeezing in a few lines before drifting off to sleep. I need to bring everything, big and small, before You and give You my burdens instead of carrying them myself. Thank You for the gift of prayer. Amen.

Ask, and it shall be given you; seek, and ye shall find;
knock, and it shall be opened unto you: for every one
that asketh receiveth; and he that seeketh findeth;
and to him that knocketh it shall be opened.
MATTHEW 7:7–8

And all things, whatsoever ye shall
ask in prayer, believing, ye shall receive.
MATTHEW 21:22

He will be very gracious unto thee at the voice of
thy cry; when he shall hear it, he will answer thee.
ISAIAH 30:19

If ye abide in me, and my words abide in you,
ye shall ask what ye will, and it shall be done unto you.
JOHN 15:7

And this is the confidence that we have in him, that,
if we ask any thing according to his will, he heareth us:
And if we know that he hear us, whatsoever we ask,
we know that we have the petitions that we desired of him.
1 JOHN 5:14–15

And it shall come to pass, that before they call, I will
answer; and while they are yet speaking, I will hear.
ISAIAH 65:24

Whatsoever ye shall ask the Father in my name, he will
give it you. Hitherto have ye asked nothing in my name:
ask, and ye shall receive, that your joy may be full.
JOHN 16:23–24

Confess your faults one to another, and pray one
for another, that ye may be healed. The effectual
fervent prayer of a righteous man availeth much.
JAMES 5:16

And I say unto you, Ask, and it shall be given you; seek,
and ye shall find; knock, and it shall be opened unto you.
LUKE 11:9

And whatsoever ye shall ask in my name, that will
I do, that the Father may be glorified in the Son.
If ye shall ask any thing in my name, I will do it.
JOHN 14:13–14

But thou, when thou prayest, enter into thy closet, and when thou hast shut thy door, pray to thy Father which is in secret; and thy Father which seeth in secret shall reward thee openly.

MATTHEW 6:6

He shall call upon me, and I will answer him.

PSALM 91:15

There is rest, sweet rest, at the Master's feet,
There is favor now at the mercy seat,
For atoning blood has been sprinkled there;
There is always a blessing, a blessing in prayer.

"A BLESSING IN PRAYER," ELIZA E. HEWITT

The LORD is far from the wicked:
but he heareth the prayer of the righteous.

PROVERBS 15:29

O thou that hearest prayer, unto thee shall all flesh come.

PSALM 65:2

The righteous cry, and the LORD heareth,
and delivereth them out of all their troubles.

PSALM 34:17

If ye then, being evil, know how to give good gifts unto your children, how much more shall your Father which is in heaven give good things to them that ask him?

MATTHEW 7:11

Then shalt thou call, and the LORD shall answer;
thou shalt cry, and he shall say, Here I am.
ISAIAH 58:9

Evening, and morning, and at noon, will I pray,
and cry aloud: and he shall hear my voice.
PSALM 55:17

The LORD is nigh unto all them that call upon him,
to all that call upon him in truth. He will fulfil the
desire of them that fear him: he also will hear
their cry, and will save them.
PSALM 145:18–19

And I will bring the third part through the fire, and will
refine them as silver is refined, and will try them as gold is
tried: they shall call on my name, and I will hear them: I will
say, It is my people: and they shall say, The LORD is my God.
ZECHARIAH 13:9

Be not ye therefore like unto them: for your Father
knoweth what things ye have need of, before ye ask him.
MATTHEW 6:8

Then shall ye call upon me, and ye shall go
and pray unto me, and I will hearken unto you.
JEREMIAH 29:12

And whatsoever we ask, we receive of him,
because we keep his commandments,
and do those things that are pleasing in his sight.
1 JOHN 3:22

Sweet hour of prayer! sweet hour of prayer!
That calls me from a world of care,
And bids me at my Father's throne
Make all my wants and wishes known.
In seasons of distress and grief,
My soul has often found relief
And oft escaped the tempter's snare
By thy return, sweet hour of prayer!

"SWEET HOUR OF PRAYER," WILLIAM WALFORD

PRIDE

Dear God, I take pride in so many of my accomplishments and do not give nearly enough credit to You. Humble me. Let me show others that my abilities and gifts come from You and that everything good in my life is a blessing You have given me. Amen.

Pride goeth before destruction,
and a haughty spirit before a fall.
PROVERBS 16:18

Woe unto them that are wise in their own eyes,
and prudent in their own sight!
ISAIAH 5:21

Seest thou a man wise in his own conceit?
there is more hope of a fool than of him.
PROVERBS 26:12

Look on every one that is proud, and bring him low;
and tread down the wicked in their place.
JOB 40:12

An high look, and a proud heart,
and the plowing of the wicked, is sin.
PROVERBS 21:4

The fear of the LORD is to hate evil:
pride, and arrogancy, and the evil way,
and the froward mouth, do I hate.

PROVERBS 8:13

But he that glorieth, let him glory in the Lord.
For not he that commendeth himself is approved,
but whom the Lord commendeth.

2 CORINTHIANS 10:17–18

When I survey the wondrous cross
On which the Prince of glory died,
My richest gain I count but loss,
And pour contempt on all my pride.

"WHEN I SURVEY THE WONDROUS CROSS," ISAAC WATTS

And he said unto them, Ye are they which justify
yourselves before men; but God knoweth your
hearts: for that which is highly esteemed among
men is abomination in the sight of God.

LUKE 16:15

Let another man praise thee, and not thine own mouth;
a stranger, and not thine own lips.

PROVERBS 27:2

Thou hast rebuked the proud that are cursed,
which do err from thy commandments.

PSALM 119:21

He that is of a proud heart stirreth up strife: but he that putteth his trust in the LORD shall be made fat. He that trusteth in his own heart is a fool: but whoso walketh wisely, he shall be delivered.

PROVERBS 28:25–26

How can ye believe, which receive honour one of another, and seek not the honour that cometh from God only?

JOHN 5:44

And he sat down, and called the twelve, and saith unto them, If any man desire to be first, the same shall be last of all, and servant of all.

MARK 9:35

If I believe that Jesus died,
And, waking, rose to reign above;
Then surely sorrow, sin, and pride
Must yield to peace, and hope, and love.

"ETERNAL POWER, OF EARTH AND AIR," ANNE BRONTË

....
....
....
....
....
....
....

PRISONERS

Lord, I am a prisoner to so many things, but most of all myself. My selfishness, fears, and anxieties hold me captive so often. . . I want to be free. Show me the way to freedom through You, Lord, and help me to choose it every day. Amen.

But thus saith the LORD, Even the captives of the mighty shall be taken away, and the prey of the terrible shall be delivered: for I will contend with him that contendeth with thee, and I will save thy children.
ISAIAH 49:25

If any of thine be driven out unto the outmost parts of heaven, from thence will the LORD thy God gather thee, and from thence will he fetch thee.
DEUTERONOMY 30:4

For the LORD heareth the poor,
and despiseth not his prisoners.
PSALM 69:33

God setteth the solitary in families:
he bringeth out those which are bound with chains: but the rebellious dwell in a dry land.
PSALM 68:6

He brought them out of darkness and the
shadow of death, and brake their bands in sunder.
PSALM 107:14

Which executeth judgment for the oppressed:
which giveth food to the hungry.
The LORD looseth the prisoners.
PSALM 146:7

Prisoners of hope, arise, and see your Lord appear;
Lo! on the wings of love He flies, and brings redemption near;
Redemption in His blood He calls you to receive:
Look unto Me, the pardoning God. Believe, He cries, believe!

"PRISONERS OF HOPE, ARISE," CHARLES WESLEY

PROTECTION, GOD'S

Heavenly Father, You are my refuge and my strength—always there when I turn to You. I need Your protection and Your strength in my everyday life, and without it I would have no hope. Thank You for Your unfailing love and protection. Amen.

The name of the LORD is a strong tower:
the righteous runneth into it, and is safe.
PROVERBS 18:10

The angel of the LORD encampeth round about
them that fear him, and delivereth them.
PSALM 34:7

For the eyes of the LORD run to and fro throughout the whole earth, to shew himself strong in the behalf of them whose heart is perfect toward him. Herein thou hast done foolishly: therefore from henceforth thou shalt have wars.
2 CHRONICLES 16:9

The LORD shall preserve thee from all evil: he shall preserve thy soul. The LORD shall preserve thy going out and thy coming in from this time forth, and even for evermore.
PSALM 121:7–8

When thou liest down, thou shalt not be afraid:
yea, thou shalt lie down, and thy sleep shall be sweet.
PROVERBS 3:24

And who is he that will harm you,
if ye be followers of that which is good?
1 PETER 3:13

The beloved of the LORD shall dwell in safety by him;
and the Lord shall cover him all the day long,
and he shall dwell between his shoulders.
DEUTERONOMY 33:12

Under His wings I am safely abiding,
Though the night deepens and tempests are wild,
Still I can trust Him; I know He will keep me,
He has redeemed me, and I am His child.

"UNDER HIS WINGS," WILLIAM O. CUSHING

He shall not be afraid of evil tidings:
his heart is fixed, trusting in the LORD.
PSALM 112:7

I will both lay me down in peace, and sleep:
for thou, LORD, only makest me dwell in safety.
PSALM 4:8

Because thou hast made the LORD, which is my refuge,
even the most High, thy habitation; there shall no evil befall
thee, neither shall any plague come nigh thy dwelling.
PSALM 91:9–10

The LORD is my light and my salvation;
whom shall I fear? the LORD is the strength
of my life; of whom shall I be afraid?
PSALM 27:1

And now in His presence I walk with delight,
And feel His protection by day and by night;
I think of the fountain so precious and free,
Where Jesus, my Savior, was waiting for me.

"WAITING FOR ME," FRANK HENDRICKS

REPENTANCE

—◆———•———◆—

*Heavenly Father, it's never easy to admit when I'm
wrong. . . I so badly want to be right all the time!
But because I'm not perfect, I know I'm often wrong.
Give me the grace and humility to admit my
mistakes and to ask for forgiveness. Amen.*

The time is fulfilled, and the kingdom of God
is at hand: repent ye, and believe the gospel.
MARK 1:15

And they went out, and preached
that men should repent.
MARK 6:12

The LORD is nigh unto them that are of a broken heart;
and saveth such as be of a contrite spirit.
PSALM 34:18

He healeth the broken in heart,
and bindeth up their wounds.
PSALM 147:3

Repent ye therefore, and be converted, that your
sins may be blotted out, when the times of refreshing
shall come from the presence of the Lord.

ACTS 3:19

But if the wicked will turn from all his sins that he
hath committed, and keep all my statutes, and do that
which is lawful and right, he shall surely live, he shall
not die. All his transgressions that he hath committed,
they shall not be mentioned unto him: in his righteousness
that he hath done he shall live.

EZEKIEL 18:21–22

For I am not come to call the righteous,
but sinners to repentance.

MATTHEW 9:13

Jesus gives us true repentance
By His Spirit sent from Heav'n;
Whispers this transporting sentence,
Son, thy sins are all forgiv'n.

"LAMB OF GOD, WE FALL BEFORE THEE," JOSEPH HART

RIGHTEOUSNESS

——◆———•———◆——

Lord, help me to be gracious and show Your
righteousness to others through my words and actions.
I desire to glorify You in everything I do. Help me to
keep You at the forefront of my thoughts at all times.
Thank You, Father. Amen.

For the LORD God is a sun and shield:
the LORD will give grace and glory: no good thing will
he withhold from them that walk uprightly.
PSALM 84:11

The young lions do lack, and suffer hunger:
but they that seek the LORD shall not want any good thing.
PSALM 34:10

The fear of the wicked, it shall come upon him:
but the desire of the righteous shall be granted.
PROVERBS 10:24

Evil pursueth sinners: but to the righteous
good shall be repaid.
PROVERBS 13:21

A good man obtaineth favour of the LORD:
but a man of wicked devices will he condemn.
PROVERBS 12:2

But seek ye first the kingdom of God,
and his righteousness; and all these things
shall be added unto you.
MATTHEW 6:33

Eternal Sun of righteousness,
Display Thy beams divine,
And cause the glory of Thy face
Upon my heart to shine.

"ETERNAL SUN OF RIGHTEOUSNESS," CHARLES WESLEY

He that trusteth in his riches shall fall;
but the righteous shall flourish as a branch.
PROVERBS 11:28

So that a man shall say,
Verily there is a reward for the righteous.
PSALM 58:11

For thou, LORD, wilt bless the righteous;
with favour wilt thou compass him as with a shield.
PSALM 5:12

He that spared not his own Son, but delivered
him up for us all, how shall he not with
him also freely give us all things?
ROMANS 8:32

Say ye to the righteous, that it shall be well with him:
for they shall eat the fruit of their doings.
ISAIAH 3:10

Surely goodness and mercy shall follow
me all the days of my life: and I will
dwell in the house of the LORD for ever.
PSALM 23:6

The man that walks in pious ways,
And works with righteous hands;
That trusts his maker's promises,
And follows His commands.

"WHO SHALL INHABIT IN THY HILL?" ISAAC WATTS

....
....
....
....
....
....
....
....

SALVATION

Lord, You are my hope and salvation. Because of You I am saved and have been given a purpose in this life. Thank You for Your selfless love and sacrifice for me and everyone else. I never want to take Your gift for granted or forget what You have done. Thank You. Amen.

Therefore if any man be in Christ, he is a new creature: old things are passed away; behold, all things are become new.
2 CORINTHIANS 5:17

For he hath made him to be sin for us, who knew no sin; that we might be made the righteousness of God in him.
2 CORINTHIANS 5:21

And you hath he quickened, who were dead in trespasses and sins.
EPHESIANS 2:1

For this is good and acceptable in the sight of God our Saviour; who will have all men to be saved, and to come unto the knowledge of the truth.
1 TIMOTHY 2:3–4

My little children, these things write I unto you, that ye sin not. And if any man sin, we have an advocate with the Father, Jesus Christ the righteous: and he is the propitiation for our sins: and not for ours only, but also for the sins of the whole world.

1 John 2:1–2

O boundless salvation! deep ocean of love,
O fullness of mercy, Christ brought from above,
The whole world redeeming, so rich and so free,
Now flowing for all men, now flowing for all men,
Now flowing for all men, come, roll over me!

"Boundless Salvation," William Booth

And you, being dead in your sins and the uncircumcision of your flesh, hath he quickened together with him, having forgiven you all trespasses.

Colossians 2:13

This is a faithful saying and worthy of all acceptation. For therefore we both labour and suffer reproach, because we trust in the living God, who is the Saviour of all men, specially of those that believe.

1 Timothy 4:9–10

But as many as received him, to them gave he power to become the sons of God, even to them that believe on his name: which were born, not of blood, nor of the will of the flesh, nor of the will of man, but of God.

JOHN 1:12–13

I am so glad salvation's free to all who will receive it,
Glad that the news was brought to me when I was lost and sad;
Praise His dear name, I can proclaim that truly I believe it,
For I am now His child, I know, and I'm so glad.

"I AM SO GLAD SALVATION'S FREE," JAMES ROWE

SEEKING GOD

Lord, I seek after so many things in my life: love, approval, appreciation from others, money. . . Seeking after You tends to fall to the bottom of the list when I'm busy or stressed. I don't want to forget that You are the most important relationship in my life, Lord. Help me to make You a priority no matter what. Amen.

The LORD is with you, while ye be with him;
and if ye seek him, he will be found of you;
but if ye forsake him, he will forsake you.
2 CHRONICLES 15:2

Sow to yourselves in righteousness, reap in mercy;
break up your fallow ground: for it is time to seek the
LORD, till he come and rain righteousness upon you.
HOSEA 10:12

But without faith it is impossible to please him:
for he that cometh to God must believe that he is,
and that he is a rewarder of them that diligently seek him.
HEBREWS 11:6

That they should seek the Lord, if haply they might feel after
him, and find him, though he be not far from every one of us.
ACTS 17:27

The LORD is good unto them that wait for him,
to the soul that seeketh him.
LAMENTATIONS 3:25

Seek ye first the kingdom, 'tis the Master's voice;
In His precious promise evermore rejoice.
All things else, His words are true, shall be added unto you.
In His precious promise, evermore rejoice.

"SEEK YE FIRST," ELIZA E. HEWITT

But if from thence thou shalt seek the LORD thy God,
thou shalt find him, if thou seek him with
all thy heart and with all thy soul.
DEUTERONOMY 4:29

The hand of our God is upon all them for good
that seek him; but his power and his wrath
is against all them that forsake him.
EZRA 8:22

For thus saith the LORD unto the house of Israel,
Seek ye me, and ye shall live.
AMOS 5:4

And thou, Solomon my son, know thou the God of thy father, and serve him with a perfect heart and with a willing mind: for the LORD searcheth all hearts, and understandeth all the imaginations of the thoughts: if thou seek him, he will be found of thee; but if thou forsake him, he will cast thee off for ever.

1 CHRONICLES 28:9

And they that know thy name will put their trust in thee: for thou, LORD, hast not forsaken them that seek thee.

PSALM 9:10

Come, ye that seek the Lord,
Him that was crucified,
Come listen to the Gospel word,
And feel it now applied;
To every soul of man
The joyful news we show,
Jesus for every sinner slain,
Is risen again for you.

"COME, YE THAT SEEK THE LORD," CHARLES WESLEY

....
....
....
....
....
....
....

SELF-DENIAL

❖━━━━━●━━━━━❖

Dear God, I know that I'm supposed to strive to please You, but I often find myself trying to please my selfish wants and desires instead. Give me the self-control to deny myself and to please You first. Amen.

Then said Jesus unto his disciples, If any man will come
after me, let him deny himself, and take up his cross,
and follow me. For whosoever will save his life shall lose it:
and whosoever will lose his life for my sake shall find it.
For what is a man profited, if he shall gain the whole world,
and lose his own soul? or what shall a man give
in exchange for his soul?
MATTHEW 16:24–26

Therefore, brethren, we are debtors, not to the flesh,
to live after the flesh. For if ye live after the flesh,
ye shall die: but if ye through the Spirit do mortify
the deeds of the body, ye shall live.
ROMANS 8:12–13

For the grace of God that bringeth salvation hath appeared
to all men, teaching us that, denying ungodliness and
worldly lusts, we should live soberly, righteously,
and godly, in this present world.
TITUS 2:11–12

Watch against thyself, my soul, lest with grace thou trifle;
Let not self thy thoughts control nor God's mercy stifle.
Pride and sin lurk within, all thy hopes to scatter;
Heed not when they flatter.

But while watching, also pray to the Lord unceasing,
He will free thee, be thy Stay, strength and faith increasing.
O Lord, bless in distress and let nothing swerve me
From the will to serve Thee.

"RISE, MY SOUL, TO WATCH AND PRAY," CATHERINE WINKWORTH

But I say unto you, That ye resist not evil: but whosoever
shall smite thee on thy right cheek, turn to him the other
also. And if any man will sue thee at the law, and take away
thy coat, let him have thy cloak also. And whosoever shall
compel thee to go a mile, go with him twain.
MATTHEW 5:39–41

And he said unto them, Verily I say unto you,
There is no man that hath left house, or parents,
or brethren, or wife, or children, for the kingdom of
God's sake, who shall not receive manifold more in this
present time, and in the world to come life everlasting.
LUKE 18:29–30

And they that are Christ's have crucified the flesh
with the affections and lusts.
GALATIANS 5:24

Shall we, to whom is given
For sin the only cure,
Vouchsafed to earth by Heaven,
While nations shall endure;
Shall we, in this her trial,
Forget our nation's weal,
Endure no self-denial,
Be wanting in our zeal?

"In Homes Where Pride and Splendor," Benjamin J. Radford

....

....

....

....

....

....

....

....

....

....

....

....

....

....

....

SELF-RIGHTEOUSNESS

Lord, help me to be self-aware enough to realize that I am not the wisest person. . .that I am not always kind or in the right. Help me to be humble and to realize that I am far from perfect. Amen.

There is a generation that are pure in their own eyes,
and yet is not washed from their filthiness.
There is a generation, O how lofty are their eyes!
and their eyelids are lifted up.
PROVERBS 30:12–13

The way of a fool is right in his own eyes:
but he that hearkeneth unto counsel is wise.
PROVERBS 12:15

Woe unto them that are wise in their own eyes,
and prudent in their own sight!
ISAIAH 5:21

Yet thou sayest, Because I am innocent,
surely his anger shall turn from me.
Behold, I will plead with thee,
because thou sayest, I have not sinned.
JEREMIAH 2:35

Seest thou a man wise in his own conceit?
there is more hope of a fool than of him.
PROVERBS 26:12

But he that glorieth, let him glory in the Lord.
For not he that commendeth himself is approved,
but whom the Lord commendeth.
2 CORINTHIANS 10:17–18

Jesus only, Jesus ever,
Jesus all in all we sing,
Savior, Sanctifier, and Healer,
Glorious Lord and coming King. . .

Jesus is our Sanctifier,
Cleansing us from self and sin,
And with all His Spirit's fullness,
Filling all our hearts within.

"JESUS ONLY IS OUR MESSAGE," ALBERT B. SIMPSON

He that is of a proud heart stirreth up strife:
but he that putteth his trust in the LORD shall be made fat.
He that trusteth in his own heart is a fool:
but whoso walketh wisely, he shall be delivered.
PROVERBS 28:25–26

For if a man think himself to be something,
when he is nothing, he deceiveth himself.
GALATIANS 6:3

Let another man praise thee, and not thine
own mouth; a stranger, and not thine own lips.
PROVERBS 27:2

Where shall my wondering soul begin?
How shall I all to heaven aspire?
A slave redeemed from death and sin,
A brand plucked from eternal fire;
How shall I equal triumphs raise,
Or sing my great Deliverer's praise?

"WHERE SHALL MY WONDERING SOUL BEGIN?" CHARLES WESLEY

....
....
....
....
....
....
....
....
....
....
....

SEXUAL SINS

———— • ————

*Lord, it's easy to think of sexual sins as being
purely physical. But I know that it all starts in
the mind. Purify my thoughts. Help me to resist
the temptation to indulge in impure thoughts and
to keep my focus on You, Father. Amen.*

Now the body is not for fornication,
but for the Lord; and the Lord for the body.
1 CORINTHIANS 6:13

There hath no temptation taken you but such as is common
to man: but God is faithful, who will not suffer you to be
tempted above that ye are able; but will with the temptation
also make a way to escape, that ye may be able to bear it.
1 CORINTHIANS 10:13

Now concerning the things whereof ye wrote unto me:
It is good for a man not to touch a woman.
1 CORINTHIANS 7:1

I say therefore to the unmarried and widows,
It is good for them if they abide even as I.
But if they cannot contain, let them marry:
for it is better to marry than to burn.
1 CORINTHIANS 7:8–9

Nevertheless he that standeth stedfast in his heart, having no necessity, but hath power over his own will, and hath so decreed in his heart that he will keep his virgin, doeth well.

1 Corinthians 7:37

Marriage is honourable in all, and the bed undefiled: but whoremongers and adulterers God will judge.

Hebrews 13:4

These are they which were not defiled with women; for they are virgins. These are they which follow the Lamb whithersoever he goeth. These were redeemed from among men, being the firstfruits unto God and to the Lamb.

Revelation 14:4

O Holy Spirit, keep us pure,
Grant us Thy strength when sins allure;
Our bodies are Thy temple, Lord;
Be Thou in thought and act adored.

"Keep Thyself Pure," Adelaide M. Plumptre

For this is the will of God, even your sanctification, that ye should abstain from fornication.

1 Thessalonians 4:3

Know ye not that your bodies are the members of Christ?
shall I then take the members of Christ, and make
them the members of an harlot? God forbid.
1 CORINTHIANS 6:15

Who can find a virtuous woman?
for her price is far above rubies.
PROVERBS 31:10

The Lord knoweth how to deliver the godly out
of temptations, and to reserve the unjust unto
the day of judgment to be punished.
2 PETER 2:9

Blessed is the man that endureth temptation:
for when he is tried, he shall receive the crown of life,
which the Lord hath promised to them that love him.
JAMES 1:12

For in that he himself hath suffered being tempted,
he is able to succour them that are tempted.
HEBREWS 2:18

For we have not an high priest which cannot be touched
with the feeling of our infirmities; but was in all points
tempted like as we are, yet without sin. Let us therefore
come boldly unto the throne of grace, that we may
obtain mercy, and find grace to help in time of need.
HEBREWS 4:15–16

Jesus sinners doth receive;
Oh, may all this saying ponder
Who in sin's delusions live
And from God and Heaven wander!
Here is hope for all who grieve—
Jesus sinners doth receive.

"JESUS SINNERS DOTH RECEIVE," ERDMANN NEUMEISTER

SHAME

—◆————•————◆—

Heavenly Father, I often feel shame for my thoughts,
words, and actions. It sometimes paralyzes me,
and I wallow in guilt and feel like I will never
be good enough. Free me from my self-imposed
prison of shame and guilt. Amen.

For the scripture saith,
Whosoever believeth on him shall not be ashamed.
ROMANS 10:11

Then shall I not be ashamed,
when I have respect unto all thy commandments.
PSALM 119:6

And hope maketh not ashamed; because the
love of God is shed abroad in our hearts by
the Holy Ghost which is given unto us.
ROMANS 5:5

For the which cause I also suffer these things: nevertheless
I am not ashamed: for I know whom I have believed,
and am persuaded that he is able to keep that which
I have committed unto him against that day.
2 TIMOTHY 1:12

Defend me, Lord, from shame,
For still I trust in Thee;
Since just and righteous is Thy name,
From trouble set me free.
O Lord, in mercy hear,
Deliver me with speed;
Be my defense and refuge near,
My help in time of need.

"Defend Me, Lord, from Shame," from *The Psalter*

As it is written, Behold, I lay in Sion a stumblingstone
and rock of offence: and whosoever believeth
on him shall not be ashamed.
Romans 9:33

Study to shew thyself approved unto God,
a workman that needeth not to be ashamed,
rightly dividing the word of truth.
2 Timothy 2:15

Let my heart be sound in thy statutes;
that I be not ashamed.
Psalm 119:80

Yet if any man suffer as a Christian, let him not
be ashamed; but let him glorify God on this behalf.
1 Peter 4:16

O why should gloomy thoughts arise,
And darkness fill the mind;
Why should that bosom heave with sighs,
And yet no refuge find?

"O WHY SHOULD GLOOMY THOUGHTS ARISE?" THOMAS HASTINGS

SICKNESS

---•---

Being sick is so discouraging, Lord. Things that were easy now take so much energy—energy I just don't have, Father. Help me to take care of myself and prioritize sleep and healthy eating. I need to take care of the earthly temple You have given me. Amen.

Is any sick among you? let him call for the elders of the church; and let them pray over him, anointing him with oil in the name of the Lord: and the prayer of faith shall save the sick, and the Lord shall raise him up; and if he have committed sins, they shall be forgiven him. Confess your faults one to another, and pray one for another, that ye may be healed. The effectual fervent prayer of a righteous man availeth much.
JAMES 5:14–16

And when he was come into the house, the blind men came to him: and Jesus saith unto them, Believe ye that I am able to do this? They said unto him, Yea, Lord. Then touched he their eyes, saying, According to your faith be it unto you. And their eyes were opened.
MATTHEW 9:28–30

Heal me, O LORD, and I shall be healed;
save me, and I shall be saved:
for thou art my praise.
JEREMIAH 17:14

Jesus, in sickness and in pain,
Be near to succor me,
My sinking spirit still sustain;
To Thee I turn, to Thee. . .

Through all my pilgrimage below,
Whate'er my lot may be,
In joy or sadness, weal or woe,
Jesus, I'll turn to Thee.

"JESUS, IN SICKNESS AND IN PAIN," THOMAS GALLAUDET

But that ye may know that the Son of man hath power
on earth to forgive sins, (then saith he to the sick of
the palsy,) Arise, take up thy bed, and go unto thine
house. And he arose, and departed to his house.
MATTHEW 9:6–7

For I will restore health unto thee,
and I will heal thee of thy wounds, saith the LORD.
JEREMIAH 30:17

And ye shall serve the LORD your God, and he
shall bless thy bread, and thy water; and I will
take sickness away from the midst of thee.
EXODUS 23:25

But he was wounded for our transgressions, he was
bruised for our iniquities: the chastisement of our peace
was upon him; and with his stripes we are healed.
ISAIAH 53:5

See where the lame, the halt, the blind,
The deaf, the dumb, the sick, the poor,
Flock to the Friend of humankind,
And freely all accept their cure;
To whom did He His help deny?
Whom in His days of flesh pass by?

"SINNERS, BELIEVE THE GOSPEL WORD," CHARLES WESLEY

....
....
....
....
....
....
....
....
....
....

SIN, FREEDOM FROM

—✦——•——✦—

*Lord, sometimes my past sins cause me to stumble.
I sometimes feel like I can never do anything
perfectly, so why should I even try? Free me from
the cycle of my sin, and show me how to believe
Your promises of forgiveness. Amen.*

Then will I sprinkle clean water upon you, and ye shall
be clean: from all your filthiness, and from all your idols,
will I cleanse you. A new heart also will I give you, and a
new spirit will I put within you: and I will take away the stony
heart out of your flesh, and I will give you an heart of flesh.
EZEKIEL 36:25–26

To him give all the prophets witness,
that through his name whosoever believeth in him
shall receive remission of sins.
ACTS 10:43

Knowing this, that our old man is crucified with him,
that the body of sin might be destroyed, that henceforth we
should not serve sin. For he that is dead is freed from sin.
ROMANS 6:6–7

Therefore if any man be in Christ, he is a
new creature: old things are passed away;
behold, all things are become new.

Once I was bound by sin's galling fetters;
Chained like a slave, I struggled in vain.
But I received a glorious freedom,
When Jesus broke my fetters in twain.

Glorious freedom! Wonderful freedom!
No more in chains of sin I repine!
Jesus the glorious Emancipator–
Now and forever He shall be mine.

"GLORIOUS FREEDOM," HALDOR LILLENAS

What shall we say then? Shall we continue in sin,
that grace may abound? God forbid. How shall we,
that are dead to sin, live any longer therein?

ROMANS 6:1–2

For sin shall not have dominion over you:
for ye are not under the law, but under grace.

ROMANS 6:14

Likewise reckon ye also yourselves to be dead indeed unto sin,
but alive unto God through Jesus Christ our Lord.

ROMANS 6:11

Lovely stream, river of life,
There you'll find freedom from strife,
Precious balm for the weary alway;
If you shall hear to believe,
Pardoning grace you shall receive,
And thro' Christ, gladness obtain for aye.

"THE STREAM OF LIFE," KATHARYN BACON

SIN, REDEMPTION FROM

Heavenly Father, I can't comprehend the washing away of my sins. . .the fact that You have delivered me from my transgressions and redeemed me with Your own blood. Help me to live every day in the freedom of that promise. Amen.

And she shall bring forth a son, and thou shalt call his name JESUS: for he shall save his people from their sins.
MATTHEW 1:21

Be it known unto you therefore, men and brethren, that through this man is preached unto you the forgiveness of sins.
ACTS 13:38

Who gave himself for our sins, that he might deliver us from this present evil world, according to the will of God and our Father.
GALATIANS 1:4

And if any man sin, we have an advocate with the Father, Jesus Christ the righteous: and he is the propitiation for our sins: and not for ours only, but also for the sins of the whole world.
1 JOHN 2:1–2

Who his own self bare our sins in his own body on the tree, that we, being dead to sins, should live unto righteousness: by whose stripes ye were healed.

1 PETER 2:24

This is a faithful saying, and worthy of all acceptation, that Christ Jesus came into the world to save sinners; of whom I am chief.

1 TIMOTHY 1:15

Redemption! oh, wonderful story—
Glad message for you and for me;
That Jesus has purchased our pardon,
And paid all the debt on the tree.

"REDEMPTION," SAMUEL M. SAYFORD

The next day John seeth Jesus coming unto him, and saith, Behold the Lamb of God, which taketh away the sin of the world.

JOHN 1:29

But he was wounded for our transgressions, he was bruised for our iniquities: the chastisement of our peace was upon him; and with his stripes we are healed. All we like sheep have gone astray; we have turned every one to his own way; and the LORD hath laid on him the iniquity of us all.

ISAIAH 53:5–6

In whom we have redemption through his blood,
the forgiveness of sins, according to the riches of his grace.
EPHESIANS 1:7

So Christ was once offered to bear the sins of many;
and unto them that look for him shall he appear
the second time without sin unto salvation.
HEBREWS 9:28

It is new, it is new every moment,
Half its marvels have never been told;
This glad message of hope and redemption,
This sweet Gospel that never grows old.

"TELL IT OVER AGAIN," A. ROSALTHE CAREY

SLANDER AND REPROACH

—◆———•———◆—

*Lord, I seek the good opinion of others daily; I want
to be liked by everyone. I know in my heart that this
isn't possible, but that doesn't make it any less difficult.
Remind me that it is really only Your opinion that
matters, and You have continually proven Your
love and acceptance of me. Amen.*

Blessed are ye, when men shall revile you, and persecute
you, and shall say all manner of evil against you falsely,
for my sake. Rejoice, and be exceeding glad: for great
is your reward in heaven: for so persecuted they
the prophets which were before you.
MATTHEW 5:11–12

If ye be reproached for the name of Christ, happy
are ye; for the spirit of glory and of God resteth
upon you: on their part he is evil spoken of,
but on your part he is glorified.
1 PETER 4:14

Hearken unto me, ye that know righteousness,
the people in whose heart is my law; fear ye not the
reproach of men, neither be ye afraid of their revilings.
ISAIAH 51:7

Lord, shall Thy bright example shine
In vain before my eyes?
Give me a soul akin to Thine
To love my enemies.

The Lord shall on my side engage,
And, in my Savior's name,
I shall defeat their pride and rage
Who slander and condemn.

"GOD OF MERCY AND MY PRAISE," ISAAC WATTS

Thou shalt hide them in the secret of thy presence
from the pride of man: thou shalt keep them secretly
in a pavilion from the strife of tongues.
PSALM 31:20

And he shall bring forth thy righteousness as the light,
and thy judgment as the noonday.
PSALM 37:6

And ye shall be hated of all men for my name's sake:
but he that endureth to the end shall be saved.
MATTHEW 10:22

Now who will bring a charge against God's chosen?
God is the One who justifies each man.
Who can condemn? Christ Jesus died for sinners,
Was raised to life, and sits at God's right hand.
From there He always intercedes for us;
None can condemn—we're justified.
He intercedes and brings our case to God;
None can condemn—we're justified.

"WHAT SHALL WE SAY?" SUSAN H. PETERSON

SUCCESS

─◆───────•───────◆─

Father God, the world has an obvious opinion of what a successful life is; but You teach the opposite of what the world says. Help me to not be distracted by what the world values and to focus more on honoring You with my whole life. Amen.

In the house of the righteous is much treasure:
but in the revenues of the wicked is trouble.
PROVERBS 15:6

By humility and the fear of the LORD
are riches, and honour, and life.
PROVERBS 22:4

And the LORD thy God will make thee plenteous in every work
of thine hand, in the fruit of thy body, and in the fruit of thy
cattle, and in the fruit of thy land, for good: for the LORD will
again rejoice over thee for good, as he rejoiced over thy fathers.
DEUTERONOMY 30:9

And also that every man should eat and drink,
and enjoy the good of all his labour, it is the gift of God.
ECCLESIASTES 3:13

Every man also to whom God hath given riches and
wealth, and hath given him power to eat thereof,
and to take his portion, and to rejoice in his labour;
this is the gift of God.

ECCLESIASTES 5:19

Then shall he give the rain of thy seed,
that thou shalt sow the ground withal;
and bread of the increase of the earth,
and it shall be fat and plenteous:
in that day shall thy cattle feed in large pastures.

ISAIAH 30:23

Praise to the Lord, who doth prosper thy work and defend thee;
Surely His goodness and mercy here daily attend thee.
Ponder anew what the Almighty can do,
If with His love He befriend thee.

"PRAISE TO THE LORD, THE ALMIGHTY," JOACHIM NEANDER

And he shall be like a tree planted by the rivers of water,
that bringeth forth his fruit in his season; his leaf also
shall not wither; and whatsoever he doeth shall prosper.

PSALM 1:3

Riches and honour are with me; yea, durable riches
and righteousness. My fruit is better than gold, yea,
than fine gold; and my revenue than choice silver.

PROVERBS 8:18–19

But grow in grace, and in the knowledge
of our Lord and Saviour Jesus Christ.
To him be glory both now and for ever. Amen.
2 PETER 3:18

For thou shalt eat the labour of thine hands:
happy shalt thou be, and it shall be well with thee.
PSALM 128:2

Come quickly in, Thou heavenly Guest,
Nor ever hence remove;
But sup with us, and let the feast
Be everlasting love.

"COME, LET US WHO IN CHRIST BELIEVE," CHARLES WESLEY

....
....
....
....
....
....
....
....
....
....
....
....

TRUST

—◦————•————◦—

*Heavenly Father, it's so easy to be cynical. . .to doubt
You when You say that You will always be there
for me, to wonder if You really will love me
unconditionally. Trust is something that takes time
and practice to develop. Please be patient with me
as I continue to learn how to trust You. Amen.*

God is our refuge and strength, a very present help in trouble.
Therefore will not we fear, though the earth be removed,
and though the mountains be carried into the midst of the sea.
PSALM 46:1–2

For the LORD God is a sun and shield: the LORD will
give grace and glory: no good thing will he withhold
from them that walk uprightly. O LORD of hosts,
blessed is the man that trusteth in thee.
PSALM 84:11–12

Trust in the LORD, and do good; so shalt thou dwell
in the land, and verily thou shalt be fed. Delight thyself
also in the LORD: and he shall give thee the desires
of thine heart. Commit thy way unto the LORD;
trust also in him; and he shall bring it to pass.
PSALM 37:3–5

Trust in the LORD with all thine heart;
and lean not unto thine own understanding.
In all thy ways acknowledge him, and he shall direct thy paths.
PROVERBS 3:5–6

Trust on! trust on, believer!
Tho' long the conflict be,
Thou yet shall prove victorious;
Thy God shall fight for thee.

"TRUST ON," ANONYMOUS

Fear not, little flock; for it is your Father's
good pleasure to give you the kingdom.
LUKE 12:32

Casting all your care upon him; for he careth for you.
1 PETER 5:7

They that trust in the LORD shall be as mount Zion,
which cannot be removed, but abideth for ever.
PSALM 125:1

Therefore take no thought, saying, What shall we eat?
or, What shall we drink? or, Wherewithal shall we be clothed?
(For after all these things do the Gentiles seek:) for your
heavenly Father knoweth that ye have need of all these things.
MATTHEW 6:31–32

Blessed is that man that
maketh the LORD his trust.
PSALM 40:4

And now that Thou dost reign on high,
And thence Thy waiting people bless,
No ray of glory from the sky
Doth shine upon our wilderness;
But we believe Thy faithful Word,
And trust in our redeeming Lord;
But we believe Thy faithful Word,
And trust in our redeeming Lord.

"WE SAW THEE NOT," ANNE R. RICHTER

WISDOM

Lord, I lack the wisdom that I need in this life. I realize that wisdom is not intelligence or knowledge but rather an understanding and realization of how much I do not know. Give me wisdom, Lord, and help me to apply it to my everyday life. Amen.

If any of you lack wisdom, let him ask of God,
that giveth to all men liberally, and upbraideth not;
and it shall be given him.
JAMES 1:5

And he will teach us of his ways,
and we will walk in his paths.
ISAIAH 2:3

I will instruct thee and teach thee in the way which
thou shalt go: I will guide thee with mine eye.
PSALM 32:8

For God giveth to a man that is good in
his sight wisdom, and knowledge, and joy.
ECCLESIASTES 2:26

I will bless the LORD, who hath given me counsel:
my reins also instruct me in the night seasons.

PSALM 16:7

Oh wisdom, precious wisdom,
We sing in praise of thee;
Thy ways are surely pleasant,
Thy works we wondering see.
There's pleasure in the seeking,
And those who seek may find,
Within thy halls of learning
A cultivated mind.

"O WISDOM, PRECIOUS WISDOM," DEBORAH BLOSSOM

Then shalt thou understand the fear of
the LORD, and find the knowledge of God.
For the LORD giveth wisdom: out of his mouth
cometh knowledge and understanding.
He layeth up sound wisdom for the righteous:
he is a buckler to them that walk uprightly.

PROVERBS 2:5–7

Evil men understand not judgment:
but they that seek the LORD understand all things.

PROVERBS 28:5

For God, who commanded the light to shine out of darkness, hath shined in our hearts, to give the light of the knowledge of the glory of God in the face of Jesus Christ.
2 CORINTHIANS 4:6

Behold, thou desirest truth in the inward parts: and in the hidden part thou shalt make me to know wisdom.
PSALM 51:6

Happy the nation whose God is the Lord;
Hearing in meekness and love
Counsels of wisdom and truth in His Word,
Looking for comfort above;
He is their rock and salvation,
He is their strength and their song,
Onward from glory to glory,
Leading them gently along.

"BLESSED ARE THEY THAT BELIEVE," FANNY CROSBY

....
....
....
....
....
....
....
....

WORD OF GOD

Lord, You have given us Your Word for a reason—so we can gain a greater understanding of You. I want to hide Your Word in my heart and to truly understand Your promises. Help me to carve out time with You and to spend time in Your Word each day. Amen.

For I am not ashamed of the gospel of Christ:
for it is the power of God unto salvation
to every one that believeth.
ROMANS 1:16

We have also a more sure word of prophecy;
whereunto ye do well that ye take heed,
as unto a light that shineth in a dark place,
until the day dawn, and the day star arise in your hearts.
2 PETER 1:19

For the word of God is quick, and powerful, and sharper
than any twoedged sword, piercing even to the dividing
asunder of soul and spirit, and of the joints and marrow,
and is a discerner of the thoughts and intents of the heart.
HEBREWS 4:12

Blessed is he that readeth, and they that hear the
words of this prophecy, and keep those things
which are written therein: for the time is at hand.

REVELATION 1:3

Search the scriptures; for in them ye think ye have
eternal life: and they are they which testify of me.

JOHN 5:39

For the commandment is a lamp; and the law is light;
and reproofs of instruction are the way of life.

PROVERBS 6:23

The entrance of thy words giveth light;
it giveth understanding unto the simple.

PSALM 119:130

The holy scriptures, which are able to make thee wise
unto salvation through faith which is in Christ Jesus.
All scripture is given by inspiration of God,
and is profitable for doctrine, for reproof,
for correction, for instruction in righteousness.

2 TIMOTHY 3:15–16

Word of God, O sacred treasure!
Sage and shepherd, king and priest,
Moved by God's own Holy Spirit,
Brought to men thy wondrous feast.

"WORD OF GOD," WILLIAM M. RUNYAN

So then faith cometh by hearing,
and hearing by the word of God.
ROMANS 10:17

As newborn babes, desire the sincere
milk of the word, that ye may grow thereby.
1 PETER 2:2

Therefore shall ye lay up these my words in your heart
and in your soul, and bind them for a sign upon your
hand, that they may be as frontlets between your eyes.
DEUTERONOMY 11:18

This book of the law shall not depart out of thy mouth;
but thou shalt meditate therein day and night, that thou
mayest observe to do according to all that is written therein:
for then thou shalt make thy way prosperous,
and then thou shalt have good success.
JOSHUA 1:8

And now, brethren, I commend you to God, and to the
word of his grace, which is able to build you up, and to give
you an inheritance among all them which are sanctified.
ACTS 20:32

Thy word is a lamp unto my feet,
and a light unto my path.
PSALM 119:105

Being born again, not of corruptible seed,
but of incorruptible, by the word of God,
which liveth and abideth for ever.
1 PETER 1:23

I do believe the Bible, the blessed Word of God,
And close unto its promises I cleave.
It points me to the pathway the saints and martyrs trod,
My Father is its author, and I believe.

"I DO BELIEVE THE BIBLE," FRANCIS A. BLACKMER

WORK

Lord, work is an essential part of life, a necessary part, and You have commanded us to work well. No matter what my position—mother, barista, or CEO—help me to work diligently and to the best of my ability. Amen.

And God blessed the seventh day, and sanctified it:
because that in it he had rested from all his
work which God created and made.
GENESIS 2:3

The LORD shall open unto thee his good treasure,
the heaven to give the rain unto thy land in his season,
and to bless all the work of thine hand: and thou shalt lend
unto many nations, and thou shalt not borrow.
DEUTERONOMY 28:12

Be ye strong therefore, and let not your hands
be weak: for your work shall be rewarded.
2 CHRONICLES 15:7

And in every work that he began in the service of the house
of God, and in the law, and in the commandments, to seek
his God, he did it with all his heart, and prospered.
2 CHRONICLES 31:21

Even a child is known by his doings,
whether his work be pure, and whether it be right.
PROVERBS 20:11

Jesus saith unto them, My meat is to do the will
of him that sent me, and to finish his work.
JOHN 4:34

Then said they unto him, What shall we do,
that we might work the works of God?
Jesus answered and said unto them, This is the work
of God, that ye believe on him whom he hath sent.
JOHN 6:28–29

I have glorified thee on the earth: I have finished the
work which thou gavest me to do. And now, O Father,
glorify thou me with thine own self with the glory
which I had with thee before the world was.
JOHN 17:4–5

To the work! To the work! We are servants of God;
Let us follow the path that our Master has trod;
With the balm of His counsel our strength to renew,
Let us do with our might what our hands find to do.

"TO THE WORK!" FANNY CROSBY

For we hear that there are some which walk among you disorderly, working not at all, but are busybodies. Now them that are such we command and exhort by our Lord Jesus Christ, that with quietness they work, and eat their own bread.

2 Thessalonians 3:11–12

Let him that stole steal no more: but rather let him labour, working with his hands the thing which is good, that he may have to give to him that needeth.

Ephesians 4:28

These words I speak, they are not just My own;
God is the One who does His work through Me.
Believe that I am in My Father God,
Or just believe the miracles you see.

"Let Not Your Hearts Be Troubled," Susan H. Peterson

WORRY

—•—

Lord, I worry about everything. What I eat,
what I will be doing in ten years, what everyone
thinks of me. . . I worry about things that I have
absolutely no control over. Whenever I worry,
help me to remember Your promises of provision
and to enjoy Your creations around me—the
animals. . .the flowers and trees. . .the world. Amen.

Be careful for nothing; but in every thing by prayer
and supplication with thanksgiving let your requests
be made known unto God. And the peace of God,
which passeth all understanding, shall keep your
hearts and minds through Christ Jesus.
PHILIPPIANS 4:6–7

God is our refuge and strength, a very present help
in trouble. Therefore will not we fear, though the earth
be removed, and though the mountains be carried
into the midst of the sea; though the waters thereof
roar and be troubled, though the mountains shake
with the swelling thereof.
PSALM 46:1–3

For he shall be as a tree planted by the waters, and that spreadeth out her roots by the river, and shall not see when heat cometh, but her leaf shall be green; and shall not be careful in the year of drought, neither shall cease from yielding fruit.

JEREMIAH 17:8

And Jesus answered and said unto her, Martha, Martha, thou art careful and troubled about many things: but one thing is needful: and Mary hath chosen that good part, which shall not be taken away from her.

LUKE 10:41–42

But my God shall supply all your need according to his riches in glory by Christ Jesus.

PHILIPPIANS 4:19

The LORD also will be a refuge for the oppressed, a refuge in times of trouble. And they that know thy name will put their trust in thee: for thou, LORD, hast not forsaken them that seek thee.

PSALM 9:9–10

Stayed upon Jehovah, hearts are fully blest,
Finding, as He promised, perfect peace and rest.
Hidden in the hollow of His blessed hand,
Never foe can follow, never traitor stand;
Not a surge of worry, not a shade of care,
Not a blast of hurry touch the spirit there.

"LIKE A RIVER GLORIOUS," FRANCES R. HAVERGAL

And we know that all things work
together for good to them that love God,
to them who are the called according to his purpose.
ROMANS 8:28

And the work of righteousness shall be peace; and the
effect of righteousness quietness and assurance for ever.
ISAIAH 32:17

Oh, glory to God! Hallelujah to Jesus!
I'm living in Canaan, the blood sanctifies.
I'm shouting the victory, while still pressing forward,
And onward, and upward, as time swiftly flies.
Temptations are many and trials are plenty,
But Jesus is with me, I'm never alone;
The Comforter fills me, my soul feels the glory,
I'm thrilled and enraptured and journeying home.

"THE CONQUEROR'S TREAD," FLORENCE POTTER

....
....
....
....
....
....
....
....
....

WORSHIP

Lord, it's so easy to think of worship as something that happens once a week in a church service, to confine it to a small area of my life. But that isn't what it should be. I want to worship You and praise You every day, for every little blessing I see. Amen.

All the earth shall worship thee, and shall
sing unto thee; they shall sing to thy name.
PSALM 66:4

O come, let us worship and bow down: let us kneel
before the LORD our maker. For he is our God; and we
are the people of his pasture, and the sheep of his hand.
PSALM 95:6–7

Now when Jesus was born in Bethlehem of Judaea in
the days of Herod the king, behold, there came wise
men from the east to Jerusalem, saying, Where is he
that is born King of the Jews? for we have seen his
star in the east, and are come to worship him.
MATTHEW 2:1–2

God is a Spirit: and they that worship him
must worship him in spirit and in truth.
JOHN 4:24

The four and twenty elders fall down before him that sat on
the throne, and worship him that liveth for ever and ever,
and cast their crowns before the throne, saying, Thou art worthy,
O Lord, to receive glory and honour and power: for thou hast
created all things, and for thy pleasure they are and were created.
REVELATION 4:10–11

All nations whom thou hast made shall come and worship
before thee, O Lord; and shall glorify thy name.
PSALM 86:9

O worship the King, all glorious above,
O gratefully sing His power and His love;
Our shield and defender, the Ancient of Days,
Pavilioned in splendor and girded with praise.

"O WORSHIP THE KING," ROBERT GRANT

Who shall not fear thee, O Lord, and glorify thy name?
for thou only art holy: for all nations shall come and worship
before thee; for thy judgments are made manifest.
REVELATION 15:4

Exalt the LORD our God, and worship at
his holy hill; for the LORD our God is holy.
PSALM 99:9

And I fell at his feet to worship him. And he said unto
me, See thou do it not: I am thy fellowservant, and of
thy brethren that have the testimony of Jesus: worship God:
for the testimony of Jesus is the spirit of prophecy.
REVELATION 19:10

And the devil said unto him, All this power will I give
thee, and the glory of them: for that is delivered unto me;
and to whomsoever I will I give it. If thou therefore wilt
worship me, all shall be thine. And Jesus answered and said
unto him, Get thee behind me, Satan: for it is written, Thou
shalt worship the Lord thy God, and him only shalt thou serve.
LUKE 4:6-8

And, behold, there came a leper and worshipped him,
saying, Lord, if thou wilt, thou canst make me clean.
And Jesus put forth his hand, and touched him,
saying, I will; be thou clean. And immediately
his leprosy was cleansed.
MATTHEW 8:2-3

I will praise the LORD according to his righteousness:
and will sing praise to the name of the LORD most high.
PSALM 7:17

And the four and twenty elders,
which sat before God on their seats,
fell upon their faces, and worshipped God,
saying, We give thee thanks, O Lord God Almighty,
which art, and wast, and art to come; because thou
hast taken to thee thy great power, and hast reigned.

REVELATION 11:16–17

Before the Lord we bow, the God who reigns above,
And rules the world below, boundless in power and love.
Our thanks we bring in joy and praise, our hearts we raise
To Heaven's high King.

"BEFORE THE LORD WE BOW," FRANCIS S. KEY